THE REKINDLED HEART

6 Essentials for Reviving Your Faith

THE REKINDLED HEART

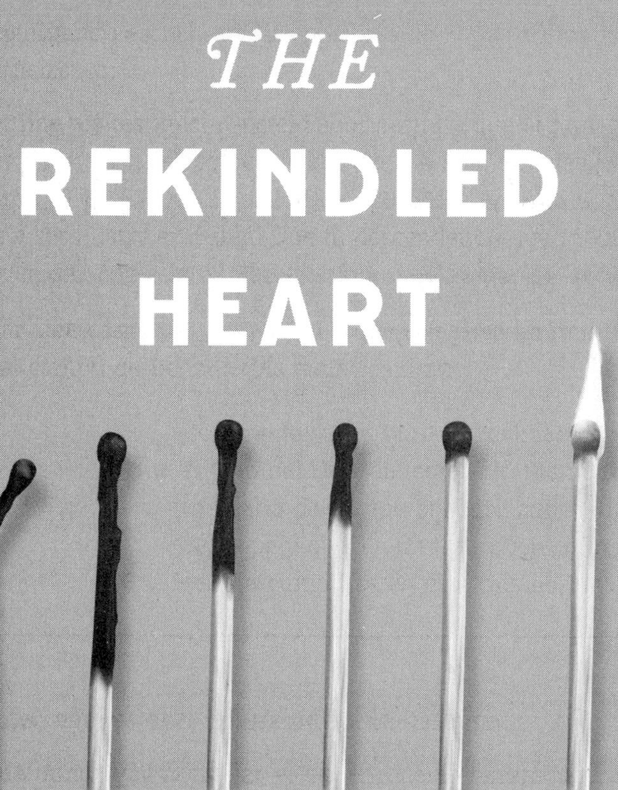

6 Essentials for Reviving Your Faith

MARK M. YARBROUGH

MOODY PUBLISHERS
CHICAGO

© 2026 by
Mark M. Yarbrough

All rights reserved. No part of this book may be reproduced in any form without permission in writing from the publisher, except in the case of brief quotations embodied in critical articles or reviews. No part of this book may be used as part of a prompt or training for AI software without permission in writing from the publisher.

Unless otherwise indicated, all Scripture quotations are taken from the Holy Bible, New Living Translation, copyright © 1996, 2004, 2015 by Tyndale House Foundation. Used by permission of Tyndale House Publishers, Carol Stream, Illinois 60188. All rights reserved.

Scripture quotations marked (NIV) taken from The Holy Bible, New International Version®, NIV®. Copyright © 1973, 1978, 1984, 2011 by Biblica, Inc. Used with permission of Zondervan. All rights reserved worldwide. www.zondervan.com

Scripture quotations marked (ESV) are from the ESV® Bible (The Holy Bible, English Standard Version®), © 2001 by Crossway, a publishing ministry of Good News Publishers. ESV Text Edition: 2025. The ESV text may not be quoted in any publication made available to the public by a Creative Commons license. The ESV may not be translated in whole or in part into any other language. Used by permission. All rights reserved.

Edited by Pamela Joy Pugh
Cover design: Graham Terry
Interior design: Koko Toyama
Cover photo of matches courtesy of uplyak/Freepik. All rights reserved.

ISBN: 978-0-8024-3771-6

Originally delivered by fleets of horse-drawn wagons, the affordable paperbacks from D. L. Moody's publishing house resourced the church and served everyday people. Now, after more than 125 years of publishing and ministry, Moody Publishers' mission remains the same—even if our delivery systems have changed a bit. For more information on other books (and resources) created from a biblical perspective, go to www.moodypublishers.com or write to:

Moody Publishers
820 N. LaSalle Boulevard
Chicago, IL 60610

1 3 5 7 9 10 8 6 4 2

Printed in the United States of America

To the memory of
Robert Charles Gilbert
"Chuck"
(1951–2021)
A man who led many to *rekindle* their faith

CONTENTS

EMBERS . . .

An Introduction

Imagine yourself in the stillness of a forest, the air crisp with the scent of pine and the earth beneath you, a dry palette of fallen leaves. The embers from the fire that burned the night before lie buried in the ashes, dormant but ready to ignite.

As twilight descends, you gather around a modest firepit with friends and family. The initial match, a mere flicker of light, catches the dry kindling and, with a gentle breath, the flame grows. And the embers from the previous night . . . the dormant coals . . . they burst to life, fueling the heat needed to catch the logs placed upon it. That small yet potent ember holds the potential to transform the cold night into a warm haven, its glow illuminating faces and kindling conversations.

As Christ followers, our faith can be vibrant, like a roaring fire.

Remember meeting the Lord for the first time? Fire.
Recall a time when God intervened miraculously? Fire.
Recount His tender leading that changed your perspective? Fire.

But our faith's flame isn't always ablaze. You and I know that to be true. Life happens, and the world takes its toll. Sometimes it's our actions. Our neglect. Our fault. Sometimes not. But before we know it, the fire that once burned brightly . . . only exists as embers below the ash. Yesterday's fire. No flame. Embers that remind us of what once was.

I think every believer has a "once was" story. I do.

I had the pleasure of growing up in a Christian home, with caring parents who lived the gospel daily. Because of God's grace, I came to faith early, carrying out a vibrant faith even as a kid. However, like many, my faith was not what it needed to be in my early high school days. Has anyone been there? It wasn't on fire. It was hidden. But a moment in my sophomore year rocked my world. A lifelong friend died in a drunk driving tragedy. He was the one who was drunk.

My pain was deep. Not only did I grieve for him and weep for his family, I had guilt. Had I been who I was supposed to be, could I have challenged him to "not run with the wrong crowd"? Would it have been possible for me to speak truth into his life and thus prevent a horror no parent and community should endure? I don't think I was wrestling with the problem of evil and the question of why God allows human suffering, but I was reflecting on my own walk of faith. I was confronted with my dormant fire, why it had become that way, and what God wanted me to do about it. That moment sent me in a tailspin that forced me to ask hard questions and to be transparent before the living God in ways I had not done before.

That's one of several stories in my life where I woke up and realized the dimness of my spiritual life. Can you relate? Our stories are unique, for sure, but they are all similar in the sense that whatever caused our moment led us to see what "once was." Well, if that is you, I have a message for you.

Take heart . . .

You can rekindle the original passion of your faith in Jesus and cause it to blaze again! The ember is there. It's just buried beneath the ashes, waiting to reignite.

This book is my sincere attempt to explore why our passion for following Jesus can fade—and to offer six essential practices that can strike a spark against the dry brush of our weary faith. My hope is to help fan that spark back into flame, rekindling a vibrant, passionate trust in the Lord. At the heart of it all, we must reconnect with the true source of our passion: Jesus.

MORE KINDLING . . .

1. How would you define what it means to be on fire for Jesus?
2. What challenges do you face in keeping your spiritual passion high?
3. What would it take to rekindle a genuine passion for Jesus in your life?

1

REKINDLED DEVOTION

Bold Trust in God's Word

"Does not my word burn like fire?" says the LORD.

JEREMIAH 23:29

If your spiritual fire has dwindled, I trust you believe there's hope for rekindling it.

Believe me, I understand how easily life can creep in and threaten to snuff out our joy. Between the daily struggle to prioritize your walk with Jesus, herding kids off to school, and doing all you can to keep the bills from stacking up, life flows on like a relentless river—always moving, never pausing. Sometimes, we're just trying to make it through the day in a draining job surrounded by difficult coworkers, feeling like we're barely staying afloat. In an ever-increasing secular culture full of ungodly patterns, we easily find ourselves failing to prioritize our Savior. Or maybe you may face some ominous physical or emotional challenges. That's all legit, I know, but I also understand that the privilege and pleasure of facing the world's chaos with Jesus is where flourishing exists. That only works if the fire of faith is on full throttle.

If unattended, the flame of faith can flicker, and you find yourself going days, possibly weeks, or longer without reading His Word or turning to Him for help. We grow accustomed to running on fumes, draining the spiritual tank to below empty. I get it. I've been there. But there is hope in the power of God's Word.

As the late Dr. Howard Hendricks, a longtime professor at Dallas Theological Seminary and one of my mentors, said so appropriately years ago: "The Bible was not written to satisfy your curiosity. It was written to change your life."

FIRST FIRE

Think back to when you first believed in Jesus. That time likely started when you encountered the truth of God through a message, a sermon, perhaps a friend's testimony, or your mother's or dad's teaching on the importance of needing a Savior. Maybe you were at camp or a youth conference, and you first felt the conviction of the Spirit to submit yourself to the living Son of God who went to the cross so you wouldn't have to pay that penalty yourself. Or, maybe you met Jesus in a hospital ward or prison. You were at rock bottom thinking, "Is this all there is?"

Whatever that experience was, it involved hearing the truth of God's Word. Without a doubt, the Spirit was at work. How God does it is always miraculous. Maybe someone spoke into your life, or you heard something that stirred your heart. However it happened, you encountered Scripture, and that encounter became the spark that ignited your faith. God's Word lit a fire in you—a desire to live for Jesus and to dig deeper into His truth through reading and study. That makes perfect sense to me, especially since we believe the Bible teaches that faith in Jesus can only be born from God's Word—igniting a flame of faith in a heart that was once spiritually dead. That's what the apostle Paul meant when he wrote,

> *So faith comes from hearing, that is, hearing the Good News about Christ.* (ROM. 10:17)

In the same way that a nonexistent faith comes to life through the power of the Word of God, a smoldering faith can be rekindled by that same power of Scripture.

I recall speaking at a church once when I noticed a man laser-focused on my words. His eyes showed he was intent on everything I said. I thought (as I was preaching!), *I wonder if he has a theological disagreement with something I have said.* But as I continued with the message, his eyes filled with tears, eventually trickling down. After the service was over and the room began to clear, out of the corner of my eye I saw him walking toward me. When he reached me, he asked a simple question: "Did someone tell you about my situation?"

It didn't take me long to realize that he was serious. I assured him that I had no idea who he was and that I had talked to no one about him. He continued, "Your words—actually, the *living words of the text* you brought forth—were for me. They cut my heart like a surgeon's scalpel." I will never forget his description, especially since he was actually a surgeon.

Now, let's make a few assessments about this scenario. Let's begin by recognizing the Holy Spirit's work before, during, and after this encounter—both in him and in me, and despite us both! But I truly cherished his words.

Don't miss it. He said it was the *living words of the text* that spoke to him. What a perfect description of Hebrews 4:12–13:

> *For the word of God is alive and powerful. It is sharper than the sharpest two-edged sword, cutting between soul and spirit, between joint and marrow. It exposes our innermost thoughts and desires. Nothing in all creation is hidden from God. Everything is naked and exposed before his eyes, and he is the one to whom we are accountable.*

My point? God's Word, engaged with a receptive heart, rekindled his buried embers. God will fire up the faith of anyone who lets Him, and one of the ways He frequently does it is through *His Word*. Christ followers believe that. We believe that the Bible is God's Word, and it is alive with purpose for our lives today. So why do we frequently forget that conviction?

CONFIDENCE IN THE TEXT

Belief in God's Word can get lost in the clutter of skepticism in our culture. The world trusts science, social structures, political regimes, humanistic philosophy, strength, power, and individual human effort. We look to medical advances and trust in technology to deliver us from every physical and spiritual malady. We write countless thousands of self-help books and pontificate about communal systems, all futilely aimed at fixing the systemic emptiness of the human soul without God. When left to themselves, every one of these entities ends in spiritual bankruptcy. They are fool's gold at best and are deceptive and destructive at worst.

Thankfully, our faith in Jesus calls us to a different conviction—to return to a bold trust in God's Word—to "trust the text," to rekindle a flickering faith.

The Christian community remains tenaciously connected to another model. Christ calls us to believe God's Word and to recommit to a bold confidence in everything God says. Why in the world would we do that? Why would we trust Scripture? Well, that's simple: We believe that Scripture is God's inspired Word. Check this out straight from the Bible:

> *All Scripture is inspired by God and is useful to teach us what is true and to make us realize what is wrong in our lives. It corrects us when we are wrong and teaches us to do what is right.* (2 TIM. 3:16)

Why do we trust the text? Because we believe it comes from the very breath of God! That's what "inspired" literally means: *God-breathed.* Friends, that phrase may be one of the most critical phrases in the Bible. All Scripture is from the very breath of God and superintended by the Holy Spirit.

When the apostle Paul wrote his letter to the Ephesian believers, he hoped to rekindle their confidence in the gospel. Many churches in Paul's day were experiencing a waning faith—their fire had begun to flicker because of attacks from false teaching and intense persecution. He didn't want them to lose their "first love." Paul was determined to refocus the Ephesians on the truth of the gospel and remind them of their first fire for Jesus. And in doing so, he reminded the Ephesians that God has spoken powerfully in His Word—and that it had changed them. Listen to his words: "And you also were included in Christ when you heard the message of truth, the gospel of your salvation" (Eph. 1:13 NIV).

That same truth can rekindle your faith, too, and bring back your fire for Jesus. Consider some fundamental truths about God and His Word.

THE WORD OF GOD IS POWERFUL

From the beginning of the story of Scripture, the biblical story flows from a singular underlying truth: The God of the Bible is a God who speaks. He has spoken. Our God is not silent. He does not speak in code, determined out of spite to keep His people in the dark. And though infinite, He is not *unknowable,* but extremely knowable through our listening to what He has said, and also by believing and trusting in what He has said!

The story of God's faithfulness is ultimately the story of His Word. From the mouths of those who have called on Him, through the voices of those He has chosen and commissioned, through the beauty of His creation, and most fully through His Son, Jesus Christ—God has graciously chosen to reveal Himself, personally and faithfully. The author of Hebrews says:

> *Long ago God spoke many times and in many ways to our ancestors through the prophets. And now in these final days, he has spoken to us through his Son. God promised everything to the Son as an inheritance, and through the Son he created the universe.* (HEB.1:1–2)

God spoke truth in so many ways before Jesus. That truth assumes that if He said it, He has the loving expectation that those who hear Him would also heed His Word. Total devotion to obeying God's truth is essential for rekindling your faith. But what are the "many ways"?

Growing up, I learned what my dad expected of me by listening to his words. Often, he would say directly, "Son, I need you to clean up your room before you head out with your friends," or "Make sure you mow the grass today. We're expecting rain." Such statements were clear as a bell, though sometimes I did not heed their clarity! In other words, through direct and plain communication, I learned to obey or face inevitable consequences (if you know what I mean).

At times, Dad also spoke in less apparent ways. He could communicate a lot through how he looked at me. For instance, when my mother talked to me, Dad's stern, tight-lipped gaze meant, "Do what your mom says, Mark." I knew *exactly* what that entailed, though he never said a word! Sometimes, he would simply smile, nod, and walk away. I felt affirmed. A "Good job, son," was embedded in that pertinent but straightforward gesture. My dad spoke in a variety of ways, but in every case, when I paid close attention and then obeyed, life went well for me. Yet not once did I doubt His compassionate love for me, or his desire for what was truly good in my life.

That is also true of our relationship as believers. As followers of Jesus, we can expect certain good things to fall our way simply by believing Him—by having faith in what He has said. Boldy believing what He says in His Word keeps our passion for Him burning brightly. Obedience stokes the fire of our faith and empowers us in our Christ-walk in a complicated world.

In addition, our faith in God's Word carries multiplying effects on those around us. It doesn't just empower us, it empowers them. Never underestimate the impact your steadfast commitment to God's Word leaves on others. I've seen younger businesspeople stand firm when they see their senior coworkers or superiors boldly affirm God's Word on an ethical matter. I've seen children empowered, even years later, when they observed a commitment to follow the Lord. On and on the stories go.

While the thrust of my discussion is focused on your faith, don't forget that your faith, fire, and embers (or tragically, lack thereof) will inevitably have far-reaching implications for those around you, either for good or for bad. Take heed, friends.

God has also chosen to make Himself known in other ways. His revelation is more than words. His Word, as critical as that may be in our walk of faith, is not the sole revelation. We serve a creative God, and He has made Himself known in what we see.

HE SPEAKS IN CREATION

God's entire story begins with a triumphantly miraculous truth as we're told in Genesis:

> *In the beginning God created the heavens and the earth. The earth was formless and empty, and darkness covered the deep waters. And the Spirit of God was hovering over the surface of the waters. Then God said, "Let there be light," and there was light.* (GEN. 1:1–3)

Everything started with God's spoken Word. He spoke the universe into existence and everything was *good*. The entire creation narrative continues the themes of God speaking and phenomenal things coming into existence . . .

> *Then God said, "Let there be a space between the waters, to separate the waters of the heavens from the waters of the earth." And that is what happened.* (VV. 6–7)

I love that. God says it, and that's precisely what happened. Over and again, God spoke a creative word and just what He commanded occurred.

> *Then God said, "Let the waters beneath the sky flow together into one place, so dry ground may appear." And that is what happened.* (V. 9)

Imagine walking out into your front yard to watch the sunrise while enjoying a cup of coffee—the dry ground under your feet feels firm because God spoke it into existence.

> *Then God said, "Let lights appear in the sky to separate the day from the night. Let them be signs to mark the seasons, days, and years. Let these lights in the sky shine down on the earth." And that is what happened.* (VV. 14–15)

If you enjoy the night sky, the shining glow of the moon, God called that into being with His Word. And that is what happened. His creative Word was not without a witness, as God declared to Job of old,

> *"Where were you when I laid the foundations of the earth [with His Word!]? Tell me, if you know so much. Who determined its dimensions and stretched out the surveying line? What supports its foundation, and who laid its cornerstone as the morning stars sang together and all the angels shouted for joy?"* (JOB 38:4–7)

Imagine God speaking all of this into existence through His mighty Word. His questions here are rhetorical. The morning stars, these mysterious celestial beings, shouted and sang for joy in response! They saw it and reveled in it. The angelic realm had front-row seats to see God's Word in action. They *responded* to His Word. God always expects a reaction to what He says. The response of praise, the response of obedience—those things rekindle the fire of our faith. Consider the psalmist David's compelling vision of God's Word in creation:

> *The heavens proclaim the glory of God.*
> *The skies display his craftsmanship.*

Day after day they continue to speak;
night after night they make him known.
They speak without a sound or word;
their voice is never heard.
Yet their message has gone throughout
the earth,
and their words to all the world. (PS. 19:1–4)

Under the vast and dark skies of Texas, one of my favorite things to do as a youngster was to look up at the sky on a clear, starry night. The vastness of that picture of God's craftsmanship mesmerized me. Though I may not have fully grasped the significance, somehow in my young heart, I heard God speak. He spoke of His power, His goodness, and faithfulness to me. I knew, somehow, that there was so much more to my life than what made me anxious. God was bigger, stronger, and more able than I to handle anything that came my way.

I still feel that way. As an avid fly fisherman, I often travel to Wyoming to fish. We camp at a canyon known as one of the physically darkest spots in the continental United States. Trust me, friends, when you step out of your tent at 1:30 a.m. and look up at the Milky Way . . . well, it doesn't whisper, it *screams*. In those moments, I feel so small—yet utterly overwhelmed that the Creator of the universe knows me and cares for me. He has allowed me to know Him. His creation doesn't just declare His glory; it confirms His grandeur and affirms His revelation. And in those still, awe-filled moments, I am empowered—because the One who made all this holds it together. Creation is God's

His creation doesn't just declare His glory; it confirms His grandeur and affirms His revelation.

shock-and-awe campaign, designed to bolster our belief in His presence and His promises.

God did the same thing with one of his chosen servants, Abraham. God had just promised Abram (his name at that time) to bless him and that He would make him the leader of a great nation. He promised as well that he would reside in a particular land that would far surpass any people group of all time. Finally, he promised that through his family line, all the world's nations would be blessed (Genesis 12). Then God used a powerful visual to drive home His Word:

> *Some time later, the LORD spoke to Abram in a vision and said to him, "Do not be afraid, Abram, for I will protect you, and your reward will be great."*
>
> *But Abram replied, "O Sovereign LORD, what good are all your blessings when I don't even have a son? Since you've given me no children, Eliezer of Damascus, a servant in my household, will inherit all my wealth. You have given me no descendants of my own, so one of my servants will be my heir."*
>
> *Then the LORD said to him, "No, your servant will not be your heir, for you will have a son of your own who will be your heir." Then the LORD took Abram outside and said to him, "Look up into the sky and count the stars if you can. That's how many descendants you will have!"*
>
> *And Abram believed the LORD, and the LORD counted him as righteous because of his faith.* (GEN. 15:1–6)

I love that story for two reasons: First—who hasn't wrestled with the desire to believe in God, yet struggled to comprehend a power so vast and limitless? Second—how excellent of God to meet us in that struggle, speaking through the overwhelming beauty of the night sky, through His creation, and even through vision, to confirm His promises and assure us of His presence. And what was the response? The Bible says, "Abram believed God." He responded in faith. Abram became a believer in that moment, but he began a deeper experience with God when he believed what He said. Then God subsequently affirmed His righteousness and lit the flame of Abram's faith.

Now, not only was Abraham (his new name) able to lead God's new nation, Israel, but he could lead and serve his family through the eyes of faith—he led them spiritually in the things of God. He could offer them wisdom that would flow from his new relationship with God. His marriage would be different, his business dealings would bear the marks of faith, and his care for those with whom he would interact on any level would be marked by his trust in God's Word. *Abram believed the Lord.* What a fabulous phrase. It was essential for becoming what God had called him to be. Incidentally, that is the only basis by which you can please God—just believe Him (Heb. 11:6).

For Abraham to become the father of God's people who would one day usher the ministry of Messiah to the world, he had to trust God's word, to believe—to trust what God said is to believe!

How does that happen? It happens, in part, as God speaks in creation. He reveals Himself through the wonder of what He has made. The response He expects is for us to believe Him. Believe His Word. Believe in His promise. Believe His goodness. That's how faithful God is to speak, as the psalmist suggests, "to all the world" through creation (Ps. 19:4).

HE SPEAKS THROUGH HIS PROPHETS

The Bible makes clear God also spoke through appointed individuals to reveal His determined plan and purposes. In the

Old Testament, God commissioned prophets to talk to His people and heads of nations that would spurn His holy rule.

The classic example of this (and one of my favorites) is Jonah—who was much more than a whale of a tale!

This is how his story opens:

> *The LORD gave this message to Jonah son of Amittai: "Get up and go to the great city of Nineveh. Announce my judgment against it because I have seen how wicked its people are."* (JONAH 1:1–2)

Not only does God speak to Jonah directly, He directs the reluctant prophet to get up and go to perhaps the most notoriously pagan city on the planet and "announce" His judgment, which included an offer for them to escape destruction if they repented and believed. God spoke to His prophet and commanded him to *talk* to the people of Nineveh, and the expected response from both was obedience.

Sadly, Jonah's initial reaction was to flee from God's presence. His unwillingness to trust God's Word brought catastrophic results. Jonah epitomized shallow devotion. That's why Jonah booked passage on a merchant ship headed in the *opposite* direction from Nineveh. However, God prepared a storm that nearly sank the ship. It would have, had it not been for Jonah owning his deed. He was cast overboard, and the waters calmed.

It took a near drowning and near death by ingestion before Jonah eventually called upon the Lord, albeit to save his life as opposed to transform his heart. From the deep, God longed for a heart of surrendered obedience to rekindle Jonah's hard heart. See the connection? Once Jonah was regurgitated onto the shores of the Mediterranean, he made his way to Nineveh. There, he preached the Word of the Lord for several days in that great city and witnessed the spark of a massive spiritual revival. When the king and the people of Nineveh heard God's Word, they were brokenhearted, and in their repentance, they were saved from impending destruction.

It's too bad Jonah never fully got it, at least not in the book that bears his name. But that generation of Ninevites sure did. You can see the transforming impact of believing God—trusting in His Word. Those people came to know Him, and calamity was avoided for approximately 150 years!

Throughout the story of Scripture, God speaks powerfully and boldly through prophets like David, Isaiah, Daniel, Zechariah, Jeremiah, Joel, Malachi, and others. Ultimately, there came a voice who would cry out in the wilderness, one foretold by Isaiah himself (Isa. 40:3), and later quoted in Mark's gospel:

> *"Look, I am sending my messenger ahead of you, and he will prepare your way. He is a voice shouting in the wilderness, 'Prepare the way for the Lord's coming! Clear the road for him!'"* (MARK 1:2–3)

A large portion of the Bible consists of God's Word spoken through the prophets of old. However, a new day would dawn eventually of God's speaking, no longer through the prophets, but through His only Son.

HE SPEAKS THROUGH HIS SON

I grew up in a wonderful Christian home. It was one of those homes where my first words were, "Mama, Dada, Jesus." Jesus was not just taught in my house, but He was lived out in very tangible ways by both of my parents. By profession, my parents were educators; my mom taught elementary school, and my father was a principal. In addition, my dad was also a bi-vocational pastor. That meant that every weekend, we would make a forty-minute drive from our house near Fort Worth, Texas, to southeast Dallas to meet with the fine folks at Prairie Creek Church.

This church had some wonderful characters and stalwart saints. Marvin Evans, a plumber, was one of the most faithful men I've ever known. He and his wife sat in the same pew at church for my entire life until they went home to see Jesus. And John and Sandra Martin sang with my mom and dad in a quartet. I can still hear John's bass voice bellow songs to the Lord.

It was a great place to grow up, learn from God's Word, and make lifelong friends, some of whom I still see regularly today. I wouldn't change that for the world.

It was also at this church that I professed my trust in Jesus. Well, to be specific, that happened in my room with my dad. As I recall, I was reading *Robinson Crusoe* (yes, a youth version), and the Lord helped me piece together the concept of being lost. That night, I got down on my knees with my dad and thanked God for providing salvation through the work of Christ on the cross. A few weeks later, I made that commitment known to my faith community at Prairie Creek. I stepped down into the slime-filled baptistry at that small country church and demonstrated my trust in the Son of God to do what I did not want to do—pay the price for my sin. Yes, it was partly fire insurance (for I had recently pondered a sermon on hell!), but I wanted to hitch my wagon to Jesus to ensure heaven. To me, it was so simple: Jesus did everything for me, a sinner. He went to the cross to take care of my problem. In doing so, He wrote a check to clear my debt, and I was simply invited to trust Him. What a deal. I simply couldn't believe it. And I couldn't get over the fact that "the offer" was available to me—and to all who believed. So, I did. I believed. I signed up for the most incredible deal ever offered. And friends—I have never once regretted it. It's worth rejoicing over . . . and even singing about. Now that old hymn of the faith made sense:

I hear the Savior say,
"Thy strength indeed is small,
Child of weakness, watch and pray,
Find in Me thine all in all."
Jesus paid it all,
All to Him I owe;
Sin had left a crimson stain,
He washed it white as snow.[1]

God's Word can rekindle dwindling faith and comfort a weary heart. It makes you appreciate the old hymns of the faith in a whole new way.

A REKINDLED EFFECTIVENESS

Paul also reminded Timothy, his coworker, and the believers at Ephesus that God's Word is valuable in rekindling spiritual *effectiveness.* God's Word, according to Paul, in 2 Timothy 3:16–17 is valuable to our faith in four specific ways:

- Teaching us the truth
- Rebuking our sinful attitudes
- Correcting our wrong thinking
- Training us in godliness

One Bible teacher put it this way: "Scripture teaches us what is right, what is not right, how to get right, and how to stay right."[2] God inspires all Scripture to help teach us what is true and make us realize what is wrong in our lives. Scripture corrects us when we're wrong and teaches us to do what is right. Our faith is rekindled when we correctly understand ourselves and our relationship to God. That first flame can be rekindled. Scripture helps us grow. It helps us mature spiritually and to see ourselves for who we are and what we are.

Paul expressed it another way at a point in Timothy's life when his faith had started to flicker:

> *This is why I remind you to fan into flames the spiritual gift God gave you when I laid my hands on you.*
> (2 TIM. 1:6)

Paul brought Timothy back to when he first believed and received a commission from Paul to serve in ministry. He took him there intentionally. I don't know the details of Timothy's conversion, but Paul alluded to it. Maybe Timothy thought back to a campfire moment or when he was reading the Torah and realized Yeshua was there all along. Perhaps it happened as he listened to a sermon, and the Holy Spirit pierced his heart. Whatever it was, Paul reminded him of a time when his faith was on fire and flourishing.

Do you remember your moment? A moment when you were on fire, it was as if God could use you to conquer the world for Jesus? A time when your faith wasn't just on fire, but it was a godly ferocious flamethrower that could melt monstrous icebergs and dislodge polar caps?

Sometimes, we must look back with a fresh commitment to seeking God in His Word. In doing so, we remember whose we are, and the promises God has given us. His Word indeed is a "lamp to our feet and a light to our path."

The psalmist David exclaimed, "Your promise revives me; it comforts me in all my troubles" (Ps. 119:50).

When the flame of David's faith started to wane, he turned

to the promise of God—the Word of God. And in meditating on it, he experienced a revival of his passion for the Lord. How great is that?

CLARITY AND FRESH FAITH

Okay, confession time! I know the rest of you don't ever do this, but I remember when I was bored out of my mind. I had finished most of my pressing tasks that day, so I started watching not just cat videos, but "stupid cat" videos on my phone.

Then I stumbled on a clip that stopped me dead in my tracks and made me weep. I came across this incredible video of a young toddler who had struggled with poor vision all her life. She simply couldn't see, or at least had horrific vision. She had been fitted with special glasses to help clear her vision, and the video captured her first reactions when she put on the new glasses.

At first, she resisted—fighting her patient mother who was gently trying to set the glasses on her face. Even after that small victory, she squirmed as her eyes adjusted to the new lenses. But then, the most amazing and heartwarming thing happened. This sweet little girl broke into a huge, goofy grin . . . and then she giggled with pure joy. She could *see*! It was one of those unforgettable moments—so beautiful, it brings tears to your eyes. I think we are somewhat like that little girl. Sometimes, the eyes of faith have grown dim by life, adversity, age, sin, or fill-in-the-blank. Somehow, some way, we don't see things as we should. But when we allow God's Word to clear all of that, it's like putting on fresh lenses and seeing God's clear, joyful vision for our lives again.

Our faith is rekindled. The joy comes back.

But there's another way a bold trust in God's Word can rekindle our faith.

REKINDLED FOR GOOD WORKS

Scripture is God's Word, which is for our growth. But our growth is due to His good work. Paul wrote,

> *God uses it [all Scripture] to prepare and equip his people to do every good work.* (2 TIM. 3:17)

Nothing is more effective for rekindling the fire of our faith than getting back to serving Christ and bringing glory to Him. They work together. We'll talk more about that later in this book. But you know it's true. When our faith wanes, we usually lose our passion for serving. Yet the opposite is sometimes true as well. Sometimes, we must serve to ignite our faith. Jesus' vision for you is that the Word of God would continually prepare and equip you to follow Him into ministry effectiveness. Serving Jesus stokes the flame of your faith!

In other words, the purpose of our spiritual growth is for God's good work, and when we do His work, the fire of our faith grows intensely. Faith and good deeds work hand in glove to keep those embers glowing and burning brightly. The apostle Paul reminds us that "we are his workmanship, created in Christ Jesus for good works (service), which God prepared beforehand, that we should walk in them" (Eph. 2:10 ESV). How about that! Believers are created to serve!

STOKING THE FIRE

Using His Word, God will begin a process of stoking the flame of your faith and rekindling your passion for Him. But here are three things you can do to begin to stoke the fire of your faith:

First, talk to the Lord. Prayer begins the process of reigniting your fire for Him. Ask the Lord to deepen your desire to seek Him in His Word. Ask Him for a burning passion for the Word that will compel you to make daily sacrifices to meet Him in the Scriptures.

Second, open your Bible. Start anywhere. Find a book or study that can guide and encourage you. Begin by reading and praying through one psalm each day. Take the time to write a psalm out in a notebook. Writing Scripture helps you slow down and reflect on each word. Then, move into one of the New Testament gospels. Mark is a great place to start: It's shorter and full of action. Before long, you'll find your passion rekindled as you engage with the words of Jesus and learn from Him how to meet people right where they are—with love, compassion, and truth.

Third, find a place in your church or a local ministry to use your gifts for Christ. All growing ministries need help. Plug in. Make yourself available. Ask the Lord to lead you to a ministry where you can grow and be effective for His glory. You will be amazed how quickly your faith will be rekindled.

MORE KINDLING . . .

1. What things keep you from being in God's Word each day?
2. Describe a time when you remember how a passage of Scripture or a study of the Word brought clarity to a situation you were struggling to manage.
3. What two things could you do today to prioritize seeking the Lord in His Word daily?

2

REKINDLED DEPENDENCE

Total God-Reliance

Keep me safe, O God, for I have come to you for refuge.

PSALM 16:1

There's a legend about a sign marking the beginning of a road that snakes across the Alaskan tundra. It reads:

> *Choose your rut: you're going to be in it for the next four hundred miles.*

If you have been to Alaska—specifically the wilds of Alaska—it's true. We have dear friends who live part of the year in the bush country outside of Fairbanks. Their place has garnered a corner of my heart that I can't fully explain. It's rough, remote, and unpredictable. Roads to their place are nonexistent, at least in the sense that we pavement dwellers would recognize as a road.

In the wilds of Alaska, ruts are more than just a metaphor; they're a reality. Once you find yourself in one, you can be stuck there for a good while. All that to say, I get the "rut" concept. To me, it's more than a notion. I grew up in the great state of Texas, where fields were filled with ruts cut into the dry landscape by countless tractors and wagons rolling across the plains.

Most times, the image of being "stuck in a rut" carries negative connotations. You know, when you're bent toward a way of thinking, have a stubborn habit, or find yourself on a relentless "treadmill" mindset that produces little hope for creativity or new adventures. That kind of rut! When used that way, it's not a good thing. It is viewed as a bad habit that needs to be broken or changed.

However, I suggest positive things can come from choosing the right "spiritual" rut, and one of those things is a rekindling of your faith. Good patterns and practices can fan the flame of glowing embers. Here's the Bible passage that comes to my mind when I think about these two ruts, one of choosing to rely on self, the other of total reliance on God. It's from Solomon, the guy in the Old Testament who tried everything to find fulfillment. In Ecclesiastes, he kept describing everything he tried as meaningless (1:2; 12:8). Essentially, he was saying, "Been there, done that, got the T-shirt, and it was useless." Nothing worked until he decided that God was the only answer. Solomon was clear: "That's the whole story. Here now is my final conclusion: Fear God and obey His commands, for this is everyone's duty" (12:13). Solomon also addressed this idea in the book of Proverbs, his other writing. It may be his most quoted proverb. He said:

> *Trust in the Lord with all your heart [spiritual rut #1]; do not depend on your own understanding [rut #2]. Seek his will in all you do, and he will show you which path to take.* (PROV. 3:5–6)

In other words, we can choose to do life with complete reliance on ourselves and our resourcefulness and see where that leads. Or we can trust the Lord for everything—in "all you do," and resist the strong urge to lean on our own sense of understanding. When we choose the "rut" of total reliance on God, He rewards us by directing our lives. It's a radical approach to life, especially in our age of shameless self-sufficiency and narcissism. Think about it. This proverb is certainly not evident in the spirit of our contemporary culture. The pattern of the world is advancement through independence. Don't misunderstand, however; I'm all about being a responsible steward and using the gifts and abilities God has given; but when we cut Him out of the equation—look out! If you are like me, that can happen even to seasoned Christ followers. Before you know it, we are self-reliant and only engage God in times of crisis. God beckons His children to frame all things in and through Him.

Such reliance on God can be found throughout the stories of Scripture, as people like you and me wrestled with the tension of being able to rely entirely on God's power and willingness to provide. People who are faithful to the Lord are people who follow the Lord. It means they pattern themselves after Him and His ways. It means they are relying on God's ways instead of theirs. What people, you ask? Flawed people. Yes, they came to a fork in the road and chose, at least at that moment, to depend on the Lord. Do that enough times, and it becomes a pattern. It's a good rut to be in. Let me give you just a few examples:

Enoch. We don't know much about him, but I love the few words that describe him. Genesis 5 said he was found "walking in close fellowship with God" (v. 24). That's a good groove to find yourself.

Joseph. He may not be the poster child for how to present dreams to your older brothers, but he had some great moments.

When Potiphar's wife hit on him, he said, "How could I do such a wicked thing? It would be a great sin against God" (Gen. 39:9). Ol' Joe was submitting to God's way, not his way. That's a good rut.

Joshua. Remember his great moment? When challenging the nation of Israel to align with God's commands, he drew a line in the sand for himself, saying, "But as for me and my family, we will serve the LORD" (Josh. 24:15). He verbally remembered the old path and said, "I'm stickin' with that pattern."

Ruth. Do you recall her bumper sticker statement? When, after the death of her husband, she was instructed by her mother-in-law to go back to her hometown, Ruth said, "Don't ask me to leave you and turn back. . . . your God will be my God" (Ruth 1:16). Ruth saw a deep rut of faith in the road ahead, and her heart stirred to walk in it and never stray.

These are just a few examples. We could also discuss Hannah, Jonathan, Jeremiah, Timothy, Peter, Paul, and Mary (not the singing group). Hundreds more could be offered. One thing is sure: Reliance on the Lord is paramount to a rekindled faith. When you have that level of dependence on the Lord, you begin to see God's power unleashed, and the flames of faith grow hotter. That's when you "feel the burn"!

A LIFE PRINCIPLE

Now, back to our primary passage: Proverbs 3:5–6. Note the first statement. It is obvious: "Trust in the LORD with all your heart." God is reminding us to trust Him. Period. As a parent of four, I did my best to teach my kids how to trust me when they were little. Now, I'm not suggesting this as Parenting 101—but hey, they were *my* kids, so I felt I was on safe ground.

Here's what I did: I'd place them on top of the refrigerator as soon as they could sit up. Yes, you heard me—the fridge. Don't be alarmed—I was right there the entire time. They'd wobble and grin, their big "punkin' heads" helping them sway as I gently balanced them. Then I'd stand in front of them with arms outstretched and say, "Jump to Daddy!" I was inviting them to take a leap of unfiltered, unbridled trust in me—knowing I was right there ready to catch them.

Each one responded differently. One was cautious, hesitant to let go. One wasn't afraid; he just liked the view from the top. And two of them leaped with wild abandon. That's when I learned—every kid is different. That early wisdom would serve me well in the years to come.

But the best part? Over time, because my children learned to trust me, they *all* eventually jumped—with joy and laughter—right into my arms. (And yes, I caught them every single time, 100 percent!) They are adults now, but they still know I'm here—and I'll always be ready to catch them as long as I can. I realize I am subject to the frailties of this life. The good news for us is that God isn't!

When we first felt the fire and passion of knowing Jesus, we trusted Him with abandon—and lived it viscerally. We'd jump from any height, confident in His outstretched arms of love. We were about all things Jesus, ready to share the gospel's Good News with a doorpost. We'd talk of Jesus with our friends, engage at church—maybe even volunteer for two shifts in the nursery. We were committed! But that spark began to erode over time, mostly because we started to trust ourselves and take a self-reliant path.

Oh, rest assured our salvation was and is intact. Jesus secured that once and for all on the cross, and He brought us into the family when we trusted Him by faith. But life and circumstances—like the ones we discussed at the beginning—can threaten our vibrancy if we are not careful. Then we can find ourselves in a horrible rut, not a good one. When that happens, before you know it, more distance separates our first love from the reality of Jesus. In other words, we find ourselves trusting "me" rather than "He." Are you there? If you assess honestly where your walk of faith is at present, has your passion for complete reliance begun to dim?

Rekindling your passion for God often begins by returning to that place where you once trusted Him fully—for everything. It's in that space of surrender that the fire of faith can burn bright again. So, let's revisit our Scripture passage together. Let's take it slowly, phrase by phrase. Maybe—just maybe—we'll begin to fan those warm embers still glowing beneath the surface, stirring them back into a flame.

EVERYTHING PLUS NOTHING EQUALS SOMETHING

Ponder our text . . .

> *Trust in the* Lord *with all your heart; do not depend on your own understanding. Seek his will in all you do, and he will show you which path to take.* (PROV. 3:5–6)

Now, if you are like me, you would admit that Scripture, at times, can be easier to understand than it is to apply. In other words, sometimes it is easy to know what a passage says and it's simply hard to do. Sometimes our walk and our talk do not match. I think this passage is one that reflects this reality.

As I studied this passage again, I asked, *How can I possess the kind of heart that trusts in the Lord, which depends on Him*? Frankly, we're all God's children sitting on top of the refrigerator. And if God is saying, "Hey, My arms are right here, trust Me," how do I rekindle that level of trust?

Recently, I discovered something that helped me answer this question. It's a formula that helps one understand the challenge of the text, both what it says and what it is asking. The formula goes like this:

"Everything plus nothing equals something."

"Trust in the Lord with all your heart" . . . That's "everything."

Trust Him with everything. The small things, the big things. The hidden things. The mundane things. The daily things. The relationship things. The money things. The emotional things. The traumatic things.

A simple dictionary search reminds us that everything means "all that exists, all that relates to a subject, all that is important, all sorts of other things used to indicate related but unspecified events, facts, or conditions."[1] Friends, I think that just about sums it up—*everything* means *everything.* Every part of your life. That's what it means to rely fully on the Lord. To trust Him with "all your heart" means holding nothing back. God is calling us to be all in—as if we're sitting on our proverbial refrigerator. There's no area of life we can withhold if we truly want to trust Him the way He asks. So, trust Him with *absolutely everything.* Don't hesitate. Leap into His arms with full confidence because He will catch you every single time.

To trust Him with "all your heart" means holding nothing back. God is calling us to be all in.

Another part of the passage works with the first but in contrast. The Lord wants you to rely on Him for everything by not relying on your strength and understanding for anything. Do you see how that works?

The way you trust Him with everything is to determine that you can't trust yourself, your wisdom, or your resolution of a particular situation, at least not without seeking the Lord. So, how do we entirely depend on Him in a given situation? It means we go to God first. Indeed, the Lord gives us godly wisdom to execute, which comes with time and maturity. But God also instructs us to counsel with other mature believers. We need to listen to their thoughts and advice. We are challenged to pray and ask for the Holy Spirit to lead us. We trust Him by going to His Word, for it is there that He often speaks if we are there to listen. That's how we trust Him with everything. Do you get it?

> *Everything (all-in) plus nothing (not by my strength) equals something.*

That's the secret to reigniting trust: surrender. The Lord longs to show Himself faithful—perfectly capable and always willing to intervene when you place everything in His hands. When you trust Him fully, the dormant embers of your faith begin to glow again. If I insert my own understanding into the challenge first, I'm no longer depending on Him. That kind of trust—the kind that leaps off the refrigerator—is *all-in* trust. That is God's invitation.

By the way, I think we have a hard time trusting the way God asks us to trust because we've been burned before. I have. Have you? We've all been burned by other people and by ourselves, so we build up defense mechanisms to protect us from further disappointment.

However, God never disappoints when we take Him at His Word. The Bible is replete with stories of His coming through when people trusted Him with everything plus nothing. When that occurs, it leads somewhere. Don't miss that last word:

Everything plus nothing equals *something.* When we do that, total trust—it puts us in a unique position. It does something.

Back to the text:

> *Trust in the Lord with all your heart; do not depend on your own understanding. Seek his will in all you do, and he will show you which path to take* (PROV. 3:5–6).

Here is the promise. Total trust means we acknowledge Him, and He promises to make our paths straight when we do so. Please note that the Lord is not promising to make our paths easy. Or pain-free. Or without challenges. He promises to make them straight. He is "straight" in contrast to crooked (the "way of the wicked," in Proverbs 4:19). The promise is that the Lord will guide the believer on life's path despite the challenges which may come. God will lead and make one's life successful—from His vantage point. That is quite a benefit that comes from total reliance on God.

BIBLE PEOPLE "ON THE REFRIGERATOR"

The story of God's people being led out of Egypt and toward the promised land is steeped in the struggle between self-reliance and wholehearted trust in God. It's dumbfounding how quickly Moses and the Israelites forgot God's mind-boggling display of power throughout all the events of their exodus from Egypt.

Having reached the plains of Moab, guided by a cloud by day and a pillar of fire by night, Moses and the people of God found themselves in need of food. God graciously provided manna, small flakes of seedlike morsels that fell literally from the sky, the exact amount to supply their daily needs. Day after day, they ate entirely by the hand of God, and they were never hungry. Early in their journey, they were totally dependent on the provision of a faithful God.

However, after a time, Moses was met by a complaining crowd of dissatisfied followers. He actually "heard all the families standing in the doorways of their tents whining." So the Bible says, "the LORD became extremely angry" (Num. 11:10).

God commanded Moses to divide the leadership into smaller groups led by seventy chosen men, respected as elders by the people. These men were to assist Moses in meeting the people's physical needs. In response to their complaints about the food supply, God told Moses He would send meat for everyone to eat, not just for a few days, but for weeks. Moses could not believe his ears. He responded to the Lord with indignance, saying, "There are 600,000 foot soldiers here with me, and yet you say, 'I will give them meat for a whole month!' Even if we butchered all our flocks and herds, would that satisfy them? Even if we caught all the fish in the sea, would that be enough?" (Num. 11:21–22).

God's response is life-changing, especially for anyone wanting to rely on Him, and not on their own understanding. He roared in response: "Has my arm lost its power? [i.e., Remember Pharaoh, the Red Sea parting?]. Now you will see whether or not my word comes true!" (v. 23). God just laid it all out on the table. The obvious answer to the rhetorical question is "No!" Then God basically tells Moses, "Just sit back and watch!"

What a question for anyone whose faith has started to flicker. Is God not powerful enough to meet your needs? Is He not able to turn your circumstances for good and to bring glory to His name? Have you walked so far away from Him that you have forgotten how He has powerfully and faithfully provided for you? Or let's just be satisfied with God's words: "Has my arm lost its power?" In other words, "Is My power limited?"

Moses and God's people found themselves stuck in a pattern of unbelief. They needed to break free from that well-worn groove of skepticism and step into the path of trust. The parting of the Red Sea was still fresh in their memory—clear evidence that God is a miracle-working God. Providing meat for a multitude was nothing for Him. But instead of remembering, they doubted. How tragic! And yet, how often we do the same. May we not forget: Radical reliance rests solely on the mighty arm of God. Period. His arm has never failed. He has proven time and time again that with Him, all things are possible (Mark 10:27).

There is no human calculation for measuring the hand of God. Yet most believe it is much easier to choose the rut of self-reliance; however, that will aways end in despair. God's call to His people is to trust Him.

What a lesson! How about you? Have you ever had a moment when God proved Himself strong? When He showed up big time? When His arm displayed power and, figuratively speaking, was present with bulging biceps and flexed tendons? You know, the kind of flex that delivers a miracle to remind you of His strength? I'm sure you've had your moment with Him, so press that recall button and remember.

WHEN IT SNOWS, IT SNOWS

One moment occurred in my life at age twelve when my family went on a skiing adventure to Colorado. It was well before the era of detailed weather radars and minute-by-minute climate reports. We made the journey from Dallas to the Texas panhandle. Upon leaving Amarillo, looking toward New Mexico and Colorado, the skies looked ominous.

Little did we know we were heading into a megastorm. It started innocently enough near the Texas state line. As we continued, it went from bad to worse. The beautiful snowflakes soon progressed into a complete whiteout. Cars stalled as the temperature dropped below five degrees. You could see no road markings or highway shoulders, and all drivers were at a loss. It was dangerous.

Within a few hours, snow drifts piled several feet high in various places along the highway. To make matters worse, windshields iced up and wiper blades froze, demanding stops about every five minutes to remove the ice by hand. Each stop was dangerous—not knowing where we were on the road, and at times, vehicles would appear out of nowhere with no warning.

After the fifth stop, my dad's hands were frozen. He said, "Mark, at the next stop, get out on the passenger side and stay close to the vehicle. Check your footing and make sure you are on solid ground. Trust me, you'll be okay. We must get the ice and snow off and get to safety. I need your help." When my dad said that, I knew it was serious.

I still remember my mom's voice—full of fear—as she said, "Bob, be careful."

As we pulled over, I was scrambling to find my gloves while my dad was already opening his door. I still remember my mom's voice—full of fear—as she said, "Bob, be careful." And then, in a moment that felt providentially timed, just as my dad closed his door, the horn of an 18-wheeler blared. Without warning, the massive truck brushed past us, clipping the outside driver's side mirror in an instant. It was that close.

My mom, my sister, and I all screamed. That moment froze in time. We were certain my dad had been struck and killed. We sat quietly for thirty seconds, which seemed like an eternity.

I still hear my sister's voice: "Oh, Daddy." And my mother's immediate prayer was, "Dear Father, give us strength." We paused. As I fumbled for the handle on the passenger side to face tragedy . . . the door opened. My father stood there completely unharmed and said, "Are you coming or not? . . . I need your help." At that moment, we almost did *not* know how to respond. Was he real? A figment of our imagination? Was this a dream? We knew he had just been hit. As you can imagine, moments later, we wept.

We are convinced God did a miracle that day. Why? My dad never saw or heard a truck. But that mirror didn't clip itself, friends. Somehow, God did something special. God flexed his muscles and saved my dad, and we will never forget it. At that moment, we had no choice but to trust the Lord, for good or bad. We had to be *all in*. There was no space for wavering, no margin for half-hearted faith. In that moment our safety, our peace, even our next breath rested entirely in God's hands. But God led us that day. We've had days with different outcomes when a miracle wasn't present. But God was still there, leading us down His path. Being all in means you trust Him with your whole heart. There is no self, there is no depending "on your own understanding." When we trust Him, we acknowledge that He is God, and we are not. He leads us down the path we must go. Does that make sense? *Everything plus nothing equals something.*

What's your story?

THE POWER OF REMEMBERING

In December of 1978, several months into my second-grade year, my elementary teacher introduced our class to Charles Dickens's *A Christmas Carol*. I can remember the opening words:

> *Marley was dead, to begin with. There is no doubt whatever about that. The register of his burial was signed by the clergyman, the clerk, the undertaker, and the chief mourner. Scrooge signed it.*[2]

Horror! Yes, early in the book, we meet the crusty, bitter, curmudgeon miser—Ebenezer Scrooge. As we listened to the opening chapters, our teacher supplemented the text with graphic pictures. These pictures only heightened our fears and anxiety about this nasty man. After a few short chapters, we kids deemed Ebenezer wicked—the enemy of anything good or right, especially Christmas. Ebenezer was someone you did not want to meet or applaud.

As I sat in church with my family the following Sunday, something sent chills down my spine. I listened in shock, horror, and disbelief as the congregation sang a song about old Ebenezer. To make matters worse, the words of this hymn wanted us to raise him and thank him for his help. We were even supposed to arrive safely at his home. How dreadful!

Thankfully, clarity came when my parents resolved many questions as the weeks unfolded. Such was my first exposure to the unique name Ebenezer. After that, the second verse of "Come, Thou Fount of Every Blessing" took on new meaning! "Here I *raise my* Ebenezer, hither by thy help I'm come"[3] (emphasis added).

Ebenezer, a word of "remembrance," is important in 1 Samuel. It is best understood in the storyline presented in 1 Samuel 4–7. That large narrative presents four significant reminders, culminating in 1 Samuel 7:12, the Ebenezer text.

Reminder #1

Trust in God, not in things that represent God.

The larger narrative begins in 1 Samuel 4 with a simple but tragic plot. Israel went into battle to fight their arch enemy, the Philistines, and lost (vv. 1–2). They tried to rally by retrieving the Ark of the Covenant to lead them into war, but they experienced even more defeat. By the end of the day, two priests were killed, and the Ark of the Covenant, *God's symbol of His presence among His people*, was captured (vv. 3–11). When Eli, the major priest in Israel, heard this shocking news, he fell backward out of his chair, broke his neck, and died (v. 18).

The most tragic thing about this episode is that Israel's spiritual decline forfeited the protection of God because they were under covenant Law. God longed for Israel to have a broken and contrite heart, a heart that trusted Him, not things that pointed to Him. Israel trusted in a symbol, the Ark of the Covenant—a gold box representing God's presence among His people. It had become an idol to them.

Reminder #2

Honor God, including things He provides that point to Him.

When the Philistines captured the Ark of the Covenant, it became a curse for them. You can find that fascinating and somewhat gross account in 1 Samuel 5. Because of that curse, the Philistines returned the Ark of the Covenant to Israel. In 1 Samuel 6, the ark was returned to Beth-shemesh. Then the Israelites disrespected God by looking inside the Ark of the Covenant, and many died as a result (6:19–20). What a tragedy for that community. Think of what happened in Israel. First, they trusted in something too much. Then, they had no respect for its holiness! They disregarded something that *was a symbol of the presence of God* and then *treated it as an ordinary object.*

Reminder #3

God delights in humility and affirms those who openly acknowledge their complete dependence on Him.

That specific community of Israel failed to honor God by disregarding what He had given them—to remind them—of Him. Because of this great calamity, they sent the ark to another community in Israel, Kiriath-jearim, where it remained in obscurity for almost twenty years. Yet it was there that "all the people of Israel turned back to the LORD" (1 Sam. 7:2 NIV). That is where the specific context of the "Ebenezer" passage begins. In 1 Samuel 7, the prophet Samuel led the people to correct their failures of the past. They had failed to trust God and honor the things of God. Samuel called the people to give their hearts fully to the Lord, to remove anything that stood in His place, and to stand ready to serve Him. As a result of hearing Samuel's message, the people met together in brokenness and recommitted themselves to Him (vv. 3–6).

Reminder #4

Remember His faithful acts today, and trust Him for His provision tomorrow.

It was during a time of rededication and renewed covenant with God that the Philistines launched their attack. Hearing of the Israelites' gathering, the Philistines secretly prepared to attack them (7:7), but Israel learned of the coming siege and, through Samuel, they *finally* cried out to God (vv. 8–9). On *that* day—the day marked with trust and humility—God fought for His people. Notice what happened: The Lord thundered against the Philistines, and the enemy went into disarray (v.10). Israel left the city of Mizpah (where the revival had occurred), and they pursued the Philistines, eradicating their threat and presence (7:11).

After the victory, 1 Samuel 7:12 says, "Samuel then took a large stone and placed it between the towns of Mizpah and Jeshanah. He named it Ebenezer (which means 'the stone of help'), for he said, 'Up to this point the LORD has helped us!'"

Notice what Samuel does. He sets up a stone between the towns of Mizpah and Jeshanah (also called Shen). Samuel's actions are purposeful—he builds a monument, a visible marker identifying what took place at that specific location. But this isn't a memorial for the dead or a monument honoring those lost in war. This stone is a "reminder" of the powerful acts of a living God, who fights for those who are His.

Placing the stone between Mizpah and Jeshanah was deeply significant. Mizpah was where spiritual renewal happened—where a revival took place and a spiritual battle was fought. Jeshanah, likely, was the location of the physical battle, where the Philistines were defeated. The Ebenezer stone was set right in the middle of these two places as a reminder of what God had done—both spiritually and physically—in connection with the hearts of His people who depended on Him. The spiritual and the physical battles are intertwined, and that stone stood as a testimony to God's work in both realms.

Samuel named the monument "Ebenezer," which means, as 1 Samuel 7:12 tells us, "the stone of help." That stone of remembrance was given a name to assist the people in recalling God's faithfulness. To them, the name Ebenezer generated thoughts of God's rescue and His intervention. This stone triggered a specific reminder of a particular help in a specific battle, at a specific time, by Israel's specific God.

After placing the stone and naming it Ebenezer, the prophet said, "Up to this point the Lord has helped us!" (7:12). It can imply a physical marker. In other words, it would say, "God helped us right here at this spot!" But it can also mean "until now." In that regard, it would imply that God helped His people up to that point. In other words, it would emphasize God's protection of the nation in fulfilling those promises He made to Israel dating all the way back to Abraham. Quite possibly, it means both. God helped them at that specific place and had led them as a nation "up to this point." It's certainly a reminder that God acts on behalf of those who are His, and His actions give confidence to future steps. God's track record of faithfulness should provide confidence for all who follow Him.

Remembering God's faithfulness humbles us as we review

overwhelming evidence of His leadership and goodness toward us. It helps us renew our commitment to radically rely on Him for all things.

What or where is your Ebenezer?

THE JESUS FACTOR

All the promises of God in the Old Testament are fulfilled in the coming of His Son, Jesus Christ. He came to bring a life of abundance to all who would receive Him by faith and obey His Word.

His debut sermon to the world laid the foundation for all He would determine to bring to anyone who chooses to follow Him and trust in His gracious provision. All that is required is a heart of genuine poverty of spirit and a willingness to transfer trust from self to Savior:

> *God blesses those who are poor and*
> *realize their need for him,*
> *for the Kingdom of Heaven is theirs.*
> *God blesses those who mourn,*
> *for they will be comforted.*
> *God blesses those who are humble,*
> *for they will inherit the whole earth.*
> *God blesses those who hunger and*
> *thirst for justice,*
> *for they will be satisfied. (Matt. 5:3–6)*

Following Jesus requires a poverty of self—a willingness to surrender one's life and rely entirely on Him, not on personal strength or resourcefulness. This kind of surrender is essential to experiencing a deeper intimacy with Christ. Throughout His ministry, Jesus consistently confronted the issues of self-trust and the fierce individualism that so often rules the human heart. Instead, He called His followers to a childlike dependence, declaring, "I tell you the truth, unless you turn from your sins and become like little children, you will never get into the Kingdom of Heaven" (Matt. 18:3). That's a call to a frontline reliance on Him for everything plus nothing, especially an eternal destiny secure in Him.

My wife, Jennifer, and I have pretty much pushed our way through all the primary child-rearing stages with each of our now-grown children. However, it's fascinating how they made their way through each passage with various levels of ease or trauma! Our goal from the beginning always was to move them along from total dependence on us when they were infants to a place in their lives when they would become more and more independent and caring for themselves. Thus, our goal was to move them from dependence to independence.

Yes, we did our part to move our kids into adulthood. But did you notice Jesus' words in the previous passage? We all are called to be in the position of a little child (i.e., "become like little children"). Have you ever wondered why we are supposed to be like little children? I've heard countless expositions of Matthew 18 regarding the call to become like little children. Well-intended teachers have said that followers of Jesus are to be like little children because, as they say, "Children are innocent!" Innocent? Seriously? Anyone who said that or believes that has not been a parent! My experience as a parent is exactly like those of other parents. We have little sinners. The Yarbroughs raised four of them. They came out of the womb as little sinners, and they displayed their stuff.

Look, friends, there is a reason parents get them into cribs with bars just as soon as possible, for that is where they belong! They came into the world with a problem. It's called sin. Sure, there is a type of naivety. Here is my point: children are not innocent; yet they are dependent. Kids live and breathe a me-first existence from the crib.

I remember it like it was yesterday—the day we brought Kayla, our firstborn, home from the hospital. As she lay there, so tiny and still, it hit me: She could do *nothing* on her own. She was in a state of total dependence. She looked to us for everything—love, food, shelter, clothing, protection. She was completely helpless and completely trusting. And that's exactly why Jesus calls us to become like little children—because children *depend*. They don't strive to be self-sufficient—they trust. And that's the kind of posture God invites us into: one of humble, wholehearted dependence on Him.

Jesus calls His followers to become less self-reliant until finally, at the highest level of spiritual depth, they have learned to rely entirely on Him. That's why it's so challenging for so many of us. It runs counter to the human rut that keeps us relentlessly striving for total independence. Christ followers are discouraged from leaning on their own understanding.

TRY THE OTHER SIDE OF THE BOAT

Sometimes, we must learn the lesson of total reliance in a very dramatic way. That was certainly true of Simon Peter. On a sunny day in Galilee, Jesus commandeered Simon's small fishing boat to use as a speaking platform from which He could address the crowds on the shoreline. What happened next sounds like a fish tale, for sure! But it's totally true . . . Luke tells it better:

> *When he had finished speaking, he said to Simon, "Now go out where it is deeper, and let down your nets to catch some fish." "Master," Simon replied, "we worked hard all last night and didn't catch a thing. But if you say so, I'll let*

> *the nets down again." And this time their nets were so full of fish they began to tear! A shout for help brought their partners in the other boat, and soon both boats were filled with fish and on the verge of sinking. When Simon Peter realized what had happened, he fell to his knees before Jesus and said, "Oh, Lord, please leave me—I'm such a sinful man."* (LUKE 5:4–8)

Ah, yes, remember? "God blesses those who are poor and realize their need for him, for the Kingdom of Heaven is theirs" (Matt. 5:3).

By God's grace, the Lord has allowed me to serve and minister to some of the country's most successful individuals in business. God has blessed these men and women with Solomonic resources and skill. Yet, a theme frequently emerges when you begin to probe their spiritual journeys. Some have learned how to run deep in their reliance on the Lord for everything. Their faith burns with a glow because they have learned the truth of God's trustworthiness.

Once they were brought to their knees in brokenness and humility, they came to fully appreciate the value of a radical reliance on God for *everything.*

As they reveal their individual story, you realize that each of them had to learn the importance of letting go of their resourcefulness before they could ever truly experience the blessings of following Christ and relying on His provision.

Some of these individuals experienced bankruptcy—some multiple times. Others lost everything because they tried to go it alone, taking risks without ever turning to the Lord for counsel or seeking wisdom from His Word. However, once they were brought to their knees in brokenness and humility, they came to fully appreciate the value of a radical reliance on God for *everything*. No matter what we have or where we stand, we are called to submit—and then to live in a position of dependence.

One way or another, it will happen. In His mercy, God gives us the opportunity to choose that path now, as His Spirit convicts and calls us to trust Him completely. You might be reading this and sense that God is speaking to you about what you have been trying to wrestle with for years. Perhaps it's the heartbreak of an adult child overwhelmed by depression, or a loved one's struggle with addiction, so painful that you haven't experienced a moment of peace in years. Maybe you have tried everything on your own to make financial ends meet, and you simply can't pull it together. You may even know that God has been calling you to obey His commands to give back to Him out of your abundance.

Perhaps your once blazing fire of faith in Jesus has started to burn out because you're weary of the fight. I get it. I have been there also. Whatever it is, the Lord may use the resulting pressure to bring you to your "other side of the boat" moment.

Try throwing your "net" on the other side of your boat. In other words, humble yourself before God, do exactly what He says, and see how He responds. If you are unsure, cry out to Him in prayer and seek Him for a season in His Word. He will hear your voice, and He will speak to your heart. He wants this much more than you do at this point. You will be glad you listened to His voice.

FAN THE FLAME: TAKE HIM AT HIS WORD

The secret to total reliance on the Lord is to take Him at His Word. Even though what He asks of you might contradict everything you have ever learned or thought, determine to do what He says. Unfortunately, we make dependence way too tricky, when all that is needed is a daily reliance on His gracious care.

When Jesus taught His disciples to pray, He emphasized the need for "*daily* bread" from God. Jesus Himself becomes the source of all we need. He said on one occasion that He was the bread of life, the living bread (John 6:35, 51). Paul wrote to the Philippians, "And this same God who takes care of me will supply all your needs from his glorious riches, which have been given to us in Christ Jesus" (Phil. 4:19). God wonderfully supplies His riches in wisdom, provision, strength, stamina, and resilience as we walk with Him facing the daily pressures and routines of life. He not only supplies, He wants to do so "infinitely more than we might ask or think" (Eph. 3:20). Total reliance is the key.

So, stoke the flame of faith . . . *Trust Him. Everything plus nothing equals something.* Okay, ready? Now jump!

MORE KINDLING . . .

1. How did this chapter on total reliance on the Lord affect you?

2. In what ways did you find yourself in the stories of people who struggled to believe in God?

3. How can you come back to a place of trusting Him with everything? What two steps can you take today to fan your flame of trust?

3

REKINDLED LOVE

Authentic Compassion for Others

Be kind to each other, tenderhearted, forgiving one another.

EPHESIANS 4:32

A while back, I read a captivating book.

I admit the book did not deliver much of substantive value to my life, but it was one of those books I found impossible to stop reading. It was filled with interesting tidbits of human facts and trivia that I find fascinating to collect. I know it sounds weird, probably is; but I was reading *Guinness World Records 2023*.[1]

Reading this book gave me a unique window into some interesting human peculiarities. For instance, I discovered that Sister Andre Lucille Rendon was the oldest person in the world, until her death in January 2023. She had lived to the fine age of 118! She was a French nun and the oldest confirmed survivor of the Covid virus (she had tested positive a month before she turned 117). What was her confessed secret to longevity? A daily morsel of dark chocolate! That's my kind of gal.

Here's another strange entry. Diana Armstrong holds the current world record for the most extended, cumulative length of fingernails. Are you ready for this? Forty-two feet and ten inches of fingernails as of March 2022, covered by the edition of *Guinness* I was reading! You should see her picture—it is stunning. I kept thinking, *How does she text on her smartphone?* Another of my favorites was the dude with the world record for the most-eaten McDonald's Big Mac sandwiches. He typically ate fourteen Big Macs each week and, according to my edition of *Guinness*, had consumed an astounding 32,672 Big Macs to that point. The longest that he had gone between eating Big Macs was eight days.

What makes the *Guinness World Records* such an engrossing read is the myriad entries of incredibly mind-blowing things people are known for worldwide. What is it that makes them distinctive? It is something special. Something unique!

When you consider what truly marks a follower of Jesus Christ, even a basic understanding of the Bible reveals this: The defining characteristic of a Christian is love. Love—now there's a word. We have been singing about love for decades. Movies swirl around love . . . and everybody craves it. But when it comes to Christians, it's their genuine love for others that is a distinctive. Love is the unmistakable hallmark of the Christian faith. It's so vital that the Holy Spirit, through Paul, dedicated an entire chapter—1 Corinthians 13—to unpack its depth and significance. And that love isn't fleeting. Its greatness endures. It abides.

Yet, when the original flame of our faith begins to flicker and fade, our passion for others often starts to wane first. We all know how easily we can douse one another's passion when we act selfishly, exert an unloving opinion onto someone else, or hurt each other by insisting on having the last word.

I've often heard people in ministry say, "Ministry would be

so wonderful if it were not for all the people!" Sometimes I can relate to that; so can you most likely. We all struggle against our selfish desires and it can be a relentless battle to love others more than we love our own agendas.

There is a better way. We can begin to fan the flame of our walk with the Lord when we ask Him to reignite our love for others. The Bible is simply filled with the concept of "one another"! God has given us the opportunity to rekindle our love and demonstrate compassion for one another.

REKINDLED LOVE: THE CALL TO LOVE AGAIN

Love is the foundation of the Christian faith. It is the defining mark of a believer and the essence of our relationship with Christ and others. Yet, love can grow cold. In the busyness of life, through hurt, disappointment, betrayal, or sheer exhaustion, the fire of love that once burned brightly can dwindle to embers. Jesus calls us back to love. It is not an option; it's a command.

I recall when our kids were small, our family tried camping. We went out with camping gear, packed the kids into the car, and off we went to the great outdoors. Everything was going well until evening, when the kids noticed all the other campsites around us had roaring campfires. The pressure was on!

Now, I learned from my dad how to stack kindling in a small triangle and then add a bit of newspaper or something to catch fire. Next, light the fire and stoke it by breathing into it, gradually adding more and more logs until the fire crackles with warmth. The only problem was that the wood I brought was still damp from rain the night before. No matter how hard I tried, I could not get that little fire to light! I could see the disappointment on my kids' faces, so I resorted to drastic measures. You guessed it: I grabbed the small can of lighter fluid and hit that smoldering fire pit with a solid dose. Bingo! It burst into a raging inferno . . . well anyway, an acceptable campfire. To my kids, I was a hero; to my wife, just another reason to shake her head.

Our faith often suffers from the same struggle to burn brightly. One reason is that our love for others has waned and become like that damp wood, keeping our faith from blazing brightly. However, a rekindled passion for others can make a difference. John 15:12–13 says, "This is my commandment: Love each other in the same way I have loved you. There is no greater love than to lay down one's life for one's friends."

Rekindling our love for others does more than restore relationships; it reignites our passion and our faith. The original passion for the Lord is rekindled when Jesus fans the flame of our love for others. Love and faith are deeply intertwined, and as we renew our love, our hearts are set aflame again with devotion to Christ. Notice the context of Christ's command to love each other. He gave that command during His discussion of what it looks like for His followers to abide or remain in Him. Remaining in Jesus means that love for Him and others is ultimately expressed in service to others.

LOVE AS THE MARK OF A TRUE DISCIPLE

Jesus made it clear that love is the defining trait of His followers. In John 13:34–35, He declares: "So now I am giving you a new commandment: Love each other. Just as I have loved you, you should love each other. Your love for one another will prove to the world that you are my disciples." This love is not a fleeting emotion but an active choice. It requires intentionality, sacrifice, and persistence. Through this kind of love, the world sees Christ in us.

John 15 continues a powerful section of Scripture known as the Upper Room Discourse. Just prior to this, we saw Jesus share the Passover meal with His disciples—a moment rich with meaning and emotion. Interestingly, Luke's gospel gives us a unique glimpse into that scene, revealing that even in such a sacred setting, the disciples were caught up in a dispute over who among them was the greatest (Luke 22:24). It's a striking reminder of how easily petty disagreements and jaded motives can smother the flame of love we're called to have for one another. Yet in the midst of that tension, Jesus modeled what it truly means to rekindle and embody genuine love. Jesus emphasized the need for His disciples to remain connected to Him, the "vine," so that they could be conduits of His love to others. Dramatically, Jesus demonstrated what that looks like:

> *So he got up from the table, took off his robe, wrapped a towel around his waist, and poured water into a basin. Then he began to wash the disciples' feet, drying them with the towel he had around him.* (JOHN 13:4–5)

This was a penetrating act of love. Jesus stooped down to wash the feet of His disciples, offering them an intimate and unforgettable expression of servant-hearted love. Can you imagine that moment? There He is, the Word in flesh, stooping to serve. Jesus, our Savior, the very Son of God, stepped into the role of a servant—a servant who was assigned to wash the feet of guests. Think of it. This is Jesus. As Colossians 1:15–16 states, "Christ is the visible image of the invisible God. He existed before anything was created and is supreme over all creation, for through Him God created everything." Jesus stepped into His creation to serve, to give His life, to lead by example. The gospel writers make this clear as they record Jesus' words: "For even the Son of Man came not to be served but to serve others and to give his life as a ransom for many" (Mark 10:45; also Matt. 20:28). That's what Jesus means when He says, "So now I am giving you a new commandment: Love each other. Just as I have loved you, you should love each other" (John 13:34). He modeled this level of love that can rekindle our faith in Him and rekindle a genuine compassion for others.

Moreover, Jesus consistently expressed His love through acts of service. He came to serve—and through His example, we are called to pour out ourselves for the sake of others. Paul echoed this truth in his letter to the Philippians, urging believers to embrace a posture of humility and selfless love, just as Christ did (Phil. 2).

THE DANGER OF A LOVE GROWN COLD

One of the great tragedies in the Christian walk is when love grows cold. It is easy to become indifferent—to let bitterness take root, hold grudges, withdraw, and choose not to forgive. That's one of the fastest ways to douse the passion of our faith. Sometimes we need a trigger to tell us how we are doing.

Okay, I admit it. I have an Oura ring. Not a mood ring(!), an Oura ring. It's a ring that tells you things about your biometrics—like sleep, temperature, stress flows, and general habits and patterns for your health. When I first got it, I thought, *I don't need a ring to tell me when I have a bad night's sleep!* But the more I got into it, I simply learned things I didn't know. For example, I never knew that I had REM patterns that dictated the kind of sleep I was getting. I had heard the acronym REM (Rapid Eye Movement) before, but didn't realize how critical it was. Nor did I know that late-night stress or food would impact my REM. Some of you may see this information in detail on your device, but it was news to me. This ring also checks my body temperature. Frequently, I will notice a rise in my temperature, which will warn me of an oncoming cold or other problems. It's fascinating.

Don't you wish you had an Oura ring for your spiritual life? One that would notify you when trouble was ahead. One that would let you know when your heart starts to grow cold. Sometimes, our love for Christ and others needs to be rekindled by Christ. The church in Ephesus received a sobering message in Revelation 2:4–5: "But I have this complaint against you. You don't love me or each other as you did at first! Look how far you have fallen! Turn back to me and do the works you did at first."

It takes work. It's the kind of work that looks like washing each other's feet—bearing one another's burdens, taking time to pray for each other, or showing compassion to someone who is hurting. And do you know what all of this takes? Time. In a busy, busy world that ramps up our pace into a frenzied existence, we frequently miss the acts of love asked of us. Not only are we robbing others of this expression asked of us, but we rob ourselves of the joy of demonstrating what God has done for us. We often forget what this pattern *does* to us. These simple but powerful acts breathe life into our love for others and reignite our faith in Jesus. Do you see how that works? Love fades if we don't tend to its flame. Left unattended, it grows cold. That's why we must be intentional in nurturing it—through kindness, forgiveness, and selfless service. Rekindling love isn't passive; it's an active, ongoing choice.

HOW JESUS REKINDLES LOVE IN US

Jesus is the source of all love. Our hearts soften when we draw near Him, and love is rekindled. We're reminded in 1 John 4:19, "We love each other because he loved us first." I appreciate how simply God's Word states such wonderful truth.

Let me suggest a few ways to rekindle that first-love flame:

Return to the source.

Spend time in the presence of Jesus—let His love wash over you. That begins by opening His Word and allowing both His truth and presence to reignite your passion for Him and for others. For many of us, this also means learning—or relearning—the discipline of being still and quiet before Him. Why is that so difficult? Because we live in a world full of noise. We are constantly bombarded by distractions—news, social media, movies, sporting events, fast-paced schedules, and on and on. I am not saying this stuff is evil. But I know this: It is all vying for our attention and pulling us away from the stillness our souls crave. There is power in silence. Learn the art of being still. Create space. Let Him speak.

Remember His love.

Take time to reflect on His sacrifice, His patience, and the grace you've experienced personally. Go back to the moment you first believed—when the weight was lifted and His love became real to you. If you keep a spiritual journal, revisit those early entries when you first trusted Jesus as your Savior. If not, perhaps now is the perfect time to write out your testimony—to remember and record the story of how He drew you to Himself. Recall what it felt like to be embraced by His love and forgiveness for the very first time. Remember His grace. The act of remembrance has the power to rekindle your heart and draw you back into the embrace of His unfailing love.

Repent of your lovelessness or lack of compassion for others.

Acknowledge where you have allowed bitterness or apathy to take hold and release it to Jesus. Remember, when you confess those sins to Him, He faithfully restores and forgives you with grace and mercy. The relief will be hard to describe as His love fills you with compassion for others again.

Renew your commitment to follow Jesus' example and serve others sacrificially.

Ask the Lord to provide opportunities to demonstrate Christlike love for someone you think may be undeserving but clearly in need of His love. You'll be amazed how quickly your passion for others is rekindled.

THE POWER OF FORGIVENESS

Unforgiveness is one of the most significant barriers to love. When we hold on to past hurts, we build walls around our hearts. Colossians 3:13 (NIV) instructs us: "Bear with each other and forgive one another if any of you has a grievance against someone. Forgive as the Lord forgave you."

Rekindling love requires that we release bitterness and extend grace just as we have received it. Are you holding on to hurt or allowing bitterness toward someone to fester? Forgiveness doesn't mean forgetting what happened. It means choosing to let go of the emotional grip the past has on you, so that healing can begin. Release it to Jesus. Ask him to bring genuine forgiveness and let go of it. As C. S. Lewis said, "To be a Christian means to forgive the inexcusable, because God has forgiven the inexcusable in you."[2] When you find this freedom, you will be able to do the following:

Invest in relationships.

Love thrives on investment. Just as a fire requires fuel, relationships require time and attention. As 1 Thessalonians 5:11 (ESV) encourages us: "Therefore encourage one another and build each other up, just as you are doing." Simple acts of kindness, words of affirmation, and intentional time spent together reignite love. Think of a couple of simple things you could do today to encourage someone—send a text, offer to meet for coffee, help someone financially, or just be available to someone for prayer. You have no idea what an impact that might have on their life.

Serve with a heart of love.

Jesus modeled love through service. He said: "And since I, your Lord and Teacher, have washed your feet, you ought to wash each other's feet. I have given you an example to follow. Do as I have done to you" (John 13:14–15). When we serve others through acts of kindness, generosity, and giving of our time, our hearts are realigned with Christ's love.

Pray for a heart of love.

Love is not just an action but a transformation of the heart. We must ask God to renew our hearts. Philippians 1:9 (NIV) says: "And this is my prayer: that your love may abound more and more in knowledge and depth of insight." Have you ever asked the Lord to rekindle your love for others? What a powerful prayer that becomes as He gently renews our passion for people. Praying for a heart that loves as Christ loves is a decisive step in rekindling passion for God and people.

THE REVIVAL OF LOVE AND FAITH

Rekindling love not only restores relationships—it breathes life back into our faith. In Matthew's gospel, the Sadducees and Pharisees asked Jesus which is the greatest commandment in the Law. Jesus was quick to answer: "'You must love the LORD your God with all your heart, all your soul, and all your mind.' This is the first and greatest commandment. A second is equally important: 'Love your neighbor as yourself'" (Matt.

22:37–39). Jesus, of course, was summarizing the Law—the Ten Commandments Moses received on Mount Sinai.

A few months ago, I stood on top of that mountain—Mount Sinai. It is beautiful. Come with me to Egypt and we will visit the Sinai Peninsula and journey to Saint Catherine's monastery and ascend that mountain and see what Moses saw. It is breathtaking. I can only imagine what went through his mind as he received from God the parameters for the nation of Israel. It had to be overwhelming.

When you look at the Ten Commandments, you discover God's heart for His people. The first four dealt with love for God, and the remaining six addressed love for others. God certainly has great concern for His children to worship Him, and Him alone. And then He also cares about how His children treat one another. He cares about community. These parameters—love God, love others—are still true today.

Love for God and love for others is at the very heart of our faith—and when that love is rekindled, so is our spiritual vitality. That's why Jesus called it the greatest commandment. When love is restored, our worship deepens, our prayers grow more alive and authentic, and the faint embers of faith ignite into a blazing fire. Love fuels our connection with God and with one another—it is the very flame that keeps faith burning brightly.

REKINDLE LOVE DAILY

Love is a choice we make daily. It isn't always easy, but it is always worth it. The apostle Paul exhorts us in 1 Corinthians 16:14: "Do everything with love." When our love begins to grow cold, Jesus gently calls us back. As we rekindle our love for others, we begin to live less for ourselves and more for those around us. This shift in perspective reorients our hearts, stirs us to love more deeply, and revitalizes our passion for Christ's mission of love.

Jesus didn't just tell us to love one another—He showed us the cost of that love. He followed His command with a powerful statement: "There is no greater love than to lay down one's life for one's friends" (John 15:13). This is love that doesn't just serve—it sacrifices. It's a love that gives not just time or effort, but everything. It's a life-surrendering love that revives our faith and draws us closer to the heart of God.

Today, we are given both the challenge and the privilege to reflect that kind of love. A love that lays aside self. A love that says, "It's not about me." Because it's all about Him—the One who is worthy of it all. We're called to lay down every part of our lives for Jesus, and in doing so, we discover the true power of love that transforms hearts, including our own.

CHESS ANYONE?

Back in the day, I played a little chess. It's a fun game. Chess is a game of strategy and patience. Multiple pieces with varying ranks of power and influence are placed on the board. The opposing player seeks to outwit the opponent with strategic moves and schemes. I'm fascinated with the individual pieces because they each have different moves and characteristics. Some are stronger, some are weaker.

Perhaps the most fascinating part of the game of chess is realizing that every piece, no matter its power or position, has one ultimate purpose. It is not to serve itself, to move because it can. Every piece exists to serve the king. Each piece moves, defends, and even sacrifices itself for the sake of the king. The king is the center of it all; everything revolves around that piece.

The same is true in our walk of faith. No matter our role or strength, our lives are meant to serve our King Jesus. When our passion flickers and our faith grows weak, we must return to Him, for He is the One who reigns in glory and provides everything we need to rekindle our love for others and reignite our devotion to His mission. He is the King who is worthy of it all. The writer of the New Testament book of Hebrews puts it this way:

> *Therefore, since we are surrounded by such a huge crowd of witnesses to the life of faith, let us strip off every weight that slows us down, especially the sin that so easily trips us up. And let us run with endurance the race God has set before us. We do this by keeping our eyes on Jesus, the champion {or King!} who initiates and perfects our faith. Because of the joy awaiting him, he endured the cross, disregarding its shame. Now he is seated in the place of honor beside God's throne.* (HEB. 12:1–2)

Friends, we are privileged because God has called us, and we have moved from death to life. If you're a Christian reading this and sense that your faith has grown dim, know this: You can return to the King of your life—Jesus—and ask Him to reignite your faith. He is always ready to restore what feels lost, and He will breathe new life into your walk with Him.

He started the work in you when you first believed, and He now desires to continue adding more and more of Himself to keep your faith burning brightly. However, you must return to the King. When others can see your trust in Jesus burning with a compassionate love for others, they, too, will be drawn closer to the King. What a beautiful picture of His grace, don't you agree?

MORE KINDLING . . .

1. What kinds of things keep you from having a genuine love for others? How would you describe your attitude toward others, especially those who may be considered "difficult"?

2. What are some examples in the New Testament where Jesus modeled authentic love and compassion for people? What kinds of responses did He receive from them?

3. List some people in your life who have been hard to love. Take time to pray for them daily and ask the Lord to rekindle your love and concern for them. Keep track in your journal of how your love for them is rekindled. Or may I be direct? Who do you need to forgive?

4

REKINDLED HOLINESS

Excellence in Character

It is required of stewards that they be found faithful.

1 CORINTHIANS 4:2 ESV

It's not about you.

You might recognize that phrase as one expression that has become part of the modern cultural lexicon.

In most cases, it's offered in jest. You deliver those words to someone who may exert too much of their opinion or agenda into a conversation or situation. Yes, I've had people use it on me before! Truth is, we all need to hear it from time to time.

The power of the phrase lies in how it exposes a shared human weakness—self-promotion at all costs. Let's be honest: It fits more situations than we'd like to admit. A spouse might say it with a knowing grin when the other bends the rules to get their way. A friend might speak it gently but truthfully when selfishness clouds a conversation. Parents say it to their children when self-interest is on full display and needs correction. From our earliest breaths, selfishness and pride seem to take center stage in our lives, revealing just how natural it is for us to seek our own way—often at the expense of others.

I was recently scrolling video clips on the "cookie challenge." If you have not seen it, this viral trend on social media is a test where parents present their small children with a situation designed to challenge their sharing and ethical decision-making skills. If both parents are involved, they sit on each side of the child. Sometimes, two children are involved. The test is simple. Each person, a child or parent, has a covered plate in front of them. On the count of three, the plates are uncovered. If two parents and a child are involved, it goes like this: One parent has one cookie, the child has two cookies, and the other parent has nothing. I must admit—it's funny to watch each child wrestle with what to do. You can see the tension on their faces. Some children share, others do not. Others look their parents in the eye and say, "I'm sorry you did not get any. That's just the way it is!" In many ways, it is a social experiment based on environment, development, shared empathy, temperament, and so on. But I know this: in real life we all fail the cookie challenge in some form or fashion. It's in our DNA. In some way, at various times and in surprising moments, we all think it is about us. It's certainly a struggle that will rear its head from time to time. Ahh, yes, the great "ME" will display selfishness.

When Jesus entered the world, He epitomized what it looks like to deny self and seek the good in every possible way to benefit others. Though it very well could have been, it was *not about Him*.

Jesus, in His own words, as we read in the last chapter:

> *For even the Son of Man came not to be served but to serve others and to give his life as a ransom for many.*
> (MATT. 20:28)

One of the most compelling New Testament passages declares this as the ultimate motivation for Jesus coming into the world as Savior. Our motivation is to do likewise:

> *You must have the same attitude that Christ Jesus had. Though he was God, he did not think of equality with God as something to cling to. Instead, he gave up his divine privileges; he took the humble position of a slave and was born as a human being. When he appeared in human form, he humbled himself in obedience to God and died a criminal's death on a cross.* (PHIL. 2:5–8)

I love that passage. Many scholars believe it was part of an early church hymn: words sung by the first believers during times of worship. Imagine that—some early church "Chris Tomlin" composed lyrics to help fellow believers remember a central truth: that we are called to be *servants*, following in the footsteps of Jesus. At its core, this hymn speaks of Christ's coming to earth and the humility that defined both His arrival and His mission. That same humility drove Him to accomplish what He did for all of us.

In those words, we find the fourth essential for a rekindled heart of faith: pursuing the service of others above ourselves. Simply put, it means choosing to live as Jesus did by becoming servants.

THE IMPORTANCE OF CHRISTIAN CHARACTER

Part of what begins to cool down our faith is a stubborn tendency to satisfy our needs or pursue gain. Let's face it, we all struggle to advance our agenda over others. We want things our way. We put ourselves before others. At times, our motivation becomes about personal gain as opposed to a heart that is motivated by service to God.

I have good news: Jesus came to conquer that in the best possible way. Heaven knows we need help. Left to itself, that tendency to serve ourselves gnaws away at everything meaningful and, in its full expression, can cause real damage not only to our self-worth but our relationships with those closest to us.

As Solomon famously observed, "Pride goes before destruction, and haughtiness before a fall" (Prov. 16:18). Sadly, we all can tell stories about how this principle certainly played out either in our life or someone's we know. Ultimately, that relentless focus on "all things me" snuffs out our passion for God and others. It diminishes the very character God calls us to reflect. The flame of faith that once burned brightly can start to fade when we take our eyes off others and turn inward instead. So, what gives? Can that be reversed?

A LESSON FROM THE DESERT

Few Christians today would question the greatness of Moses as a model of genuine faithfulness. He stands tall in Scripture as a powerful example of a life devoted to believing in God and serving Him with humility through every high and low. In Matthew's Gospel he is even seen standing with Christ Himself on the Mount of Transfiguration (Matt. 17:3).

True greatness in the kingdom of God is not about natural ability—it's about surrendered character.

But that level of faithfulness didn't come automatically. It was forged over time through trials, failures, and God's refining work. Moses' story reminds us that the character God desires to build in us often begins in weakness, not strength. His early reluctance, self-doubt, and even missteps didn't disqualify him; rather, they became the very ground where God shaped the character of a servant-leader. In Moses, we see that true greatness in the kingdom of God is not about natural ability—it's about surrendered character. Early in his life Moses, though raised to fear the Lord, trusted more in himself and his resourcefulness than reliance on God and His purposes. That self-reliance cost him nearly forty years of his life because of his impulsive and explosive actions. Remember the story?

Living a privileged life in Pharaoh's house did little to fan the flame of Moses' faith in God. Instead, it caused him to falsely believe he was his own god—a determiner of his destiny. I can't fully prove it to you, but it is possible that luxurious living may have clouded his judgment, especially on one occasion. Moses' people, the Jews, had been enslaved in Egypt since their exile years before his birth. They struggled against Pharaoh's relentless rule, and they longed for the Lord's deliverance.

The Jews' plight spanned several centuries, and tensions were intensifying as their population continued to swell. Pharaoh's horrifying attempt to quell this surge in the Hebrew population by ordering all newborn Jewish males to be drowned in the Nile River only exacerbated the already boiling emotion present among God's people. Moses' mother, trusting in the Lord's sovereign protection, hid Moses in the reeds of the Nile River by placing him in a small floating basket.

God must have heard that sweet mother's prayer, as Pharaoh's daughter discovered the young Hebrew child. The Princess brought him into the palace to raise him as her own. She named him *Moses,* the Hebrew name for "drawn out of the water."

Years later, Moses—the once proud prince of Egypt— could no longer bear to watch his people suffer under Pharaoh's relentless oppression. In a moment of heated passion, relying solely on his own strength, he took matters into his own hands—literally.

Ever been there? Have you felt the weight of consequences after trying to control your circumstances while leaving God entirely out of the equation? The temptation to pursue our glory over the Father's will can be strong. However, when we do, we stray from the character God calls us to—one marked by humility, trust, and obedience.

From Abraham and Sarah attempting to manipulate God's promise, to Samson's unchecked anger, to Jonah's defiant flight from God's call, the Bible is filled with cautionary tales of what happens when we try to "play God" with our lives. The results are never good. I know what that feels like. And I'm willing to bet you have too.

Moses' story is a compelling example of what happens when we act apart from God's timing and wisdom. As believers, our character should be shaped by obedient trust—faith that submits to His perfect, sovereign plan, and hearts that give Him the glory, not ourselves.

> *Many years later, when Moses had grown up, he went out to visit his own people, the Hebrews, and he saw how hard they were forced to work. During his visit, he saw an Egyptian beating one of his fellow Hebrews. After looking in all directions to make sure no one was watching, Moses killed the Egyptian and hid the body in the sand.*
>
> *The next day, when Moses went out to visit his people again, he saw two Hebrew men fighting. "Why are you beating up your friend?" Moses said to the one who had started the fight.*
>
> *The man replied, "Who appointed you to be our prince and judge? Are you going to kill me as you killed that Egyptian yesterday?"*
>
> *Then Moses was afraid, thinking, "Everyone knows what I did." And sure enough, Pharaoh heard what had*

> *happened, and he tried to kill Moses. But Moses fled from Pharaoh and went to live in the land of Midian.*
> (EX. 2:11–15)

What a turn of events!

In almost a moment, Moses went from prince to pauper, from the palace of Pharaoh to the desert of Midian! Or, as someone said, "From the big house to the outhouse." Moses suffered the consequences of his actions. But was he called to kill a guard? One thing is for sure. His actions led him to flee and live in the wilderness.

Sometimes we create our messes . . . and sometimes messes are simply made for us.

In God's providence, Moses was grafted into the family of a desert bedouin priest, was given in marriage to one of his daughters, and served the next forty years tending his father-in-law's herd of sheep!

We can only assume disillusionment set in as Moses wrestled with his faith through those first ten years. But what about after the second decade, the third—the fourth? Unattended, our faith easily can begin to dull as life and circumstance, sin and pressure, each take their toll on our faith. Sometimes we create our messes . . . and sometimes messes are simply made for us. They are waiting for us in this Genesis 3 world full of sin with all its ramifications. If we are not careful, it can suck the life out of our spiritual journey. We can find ourselves inwardly focused, sulking in our circumstances, and claiming that our perceived "rights" and assumed privileges have been denied. In a nutshell, making it all about us.

Sometimes, God has to rattle our cage to get our attention. Perhaps that has happened to you. I know it has happened to me. I recall a dry spiritual season—when things were hard, and the hits kept coming. Eventually, it all came to a head when we moved in the spring of 2002. We had been living in a 900-square-foot home with one tiny bathroom when child number four arrived. We had outgrown our home. And so we said a short, simple, sweet prayer: "Lord help." In His kindness, God provided a new home, and we moved from east of downtown Dallas to the home of the fighting jackrabbits, also known as Forney, Texas. Things were financially tight at that time, so I refused to pay someone to make this move for us. I ordered an 18-foot rental truck for the move, scheduled appropriately in advance. Friends, I had drawings and plans. I knew the route from the old house to the new house. I had it all organized. The move was set. My organized plans were a work of art. I was ready to go.

But the words of Scottish poet Robert Burns come to mind. "The best-laid plans of mice and men often go awry."[1] You see, the chaos started on the morning of the move. I arrived at the truck rental center to pick up the 18-foot truck I had reserved two weeks in advance. I showed up, and I walked up to the counter. I said my name is Mark Yarbrough, and I'm here to pick up my 18-foot truck. The employee stared at his computer helplessly. I have learned through the years that whenever an attendant stares at the computer, it's never a good sign.

As you've already guessed, he could not find a reservation for Mark Yarbrough anywhere. I said, "Look, I've got one friend and one day to do this. I have diagrams, I have plans, I'm organized, I must have my truck." Soon, the manager came out and said, "Unfortunately, we don't have your reservation, and we don't have an 18-foot truck available. However, one truck in the back is ready if you want it."

At that stage, I would take anything that was a truck! After signing the paperwork, we walked outside. The manager described this truck to me as we walked toward it. It was not an 18-foot-long truck; it was a 26-foot-long truck! It wasn't automatic (as I had reserved); it was a standard shift. Despite this, I had no choice but to move forward.

As I hopped up into the truck cab, the manager spoke again. He said, "You need to know a couple of things about this truck. One thing is that it rides rough." I remember asking him, "How rough?" He replied, "You'll find out." He said, "The other thing you need to know is that it sometimes slips out of second gear." I thought *How? Why? This is a moving truck.* However, I didn't have any time to waste, so I took the truck and conquered the great move.

For the most part, the day was seamless. The truck did ride rough, but I didn't notice it at first because we were getting the work done! We made three trips back and forth from one house to the other until everything had been moved. Then, on the next to last run, I noticed the truck started to shake. It was jerking everywhere, up and down, and I thought we wouldn't make it, but we did.

After emptying the final load, I said goodbye to my friend who was helping me. I called my father and asked him to pick me up at the truck rental center. I would then ride with him to a leadership meeting at church that night. I thought we'd made it.

Traveling alone in the truck, about eight miles from the rental center—that's when it happened. The truck *exploded.* Seriously. The engine blew up. It was the loudest noise I'd ever heard. We're talking flames and smoke coming out from underneath the hood. The smoke was coming into the cab. I was looking around for blood because I thought I'd been shot. The truck completely lost power, so I coasted over to the side of the road.

It was almost dark by then, but the smoke motivated me to move quickly. So, I got out of the truck and stared at the flames, which fortunately had started to subside. After a few minutes, I crawled back into the cab to retrieve my cellphone, only to discover I had left it at the new house. There I was, on the side of the highway, with no way to contact anyone. It was then that I saw some mini warehouses across the shoulder and the service road. I thought, *There's bound to be a phone in there I can use to make a call.* Fortunately, my calling card was in my wallet, so I walked to the mini warehouses, but there was no phone in sight. However, beside the mini warehouses was a sleazebucket motel—a place you did not want to be, especially after dark! And adjoining the hotel was Uncle Herman's Club.

I was still shaking from the traumatic event that had recently transpired. Then I heard a woman whisper, "Hey there, big fella."

I had no choice. I walked into the motel lobby and told them I was looking for a phone. I was told there was a pay phone in the hallway connecting the motel to Uncle Herman's Club. So, I walked down a long, dark hallway toward Uncle Herman's Club until I found it. As I stood there, I was still shaking from the traumatic event that had recently transpired. Exhausted, I leaned against the pay phone, punched in all the numbers, told the story to my dad, and asked him to come pick me up (yes, at Uncle Herman's Club).

As I hung up, I felt an arm slide around my neck from behind as I heard a woman whisper, "Hey there, big fella." Friends, I turned, and standing within twelve inches of my face—totally in my personal space—were two "women of the street." They were dressed in women of the street attire. At that moment, the only thing that I could think of to say was, "Don't touch me!" Can you believe it? But alas, it was about to go from bad to worse!

As I started to realize what was happening, I noticed the two women glance down the hallway behind me. Their sudden shift in focus piqued my curiosity, so I turned to see what had caught their attention. Coming toward us were two Dallas police officers. In my naïveté, I felt a flicker of relief. *Finally,* I thought, *someone who can help.* But that's not why they were there. Their faces were serious. Their posture was firm. They weren't coming to rescue anyone—they had other thoughts, other plans. As they approached, one of them spoke the words I'll never forget: They said, "Everyone put your hands up against the wall."

If you've never heard those words spoken to you, here is what happens: You start to do irrational things. I started mumbling. I said, "Umm, officer, I work at Dallas Theological Seminary, and I'm a pastor at a church and an elder. I like the Bible." Somewhere in my fluttered rambling, I also said "I love my wife!"

The police officer said, "Yeah, I've heard that before." I must admit I thought, *From whom?* I then made a big mistake. I had the bright idea of putting my hand down in my pocket to pull out my receipt from the truck. I could then state my case of how I didn't know these two women. Bad mistake! When I took my hand off the wall and put it in my pocket, I found my face up against the wall!

It was a horrible moment.

I'll return to finish that story near the end of the chapter. Now, I want to ask you: Have you ever been there? Okay, I'm not talking about this exact crisis, but I'm talking about that moment when the wheels come off and you find yourself in the spiritual desert. You know the moment—when your character is under pressure, and the embers of your faith are so faint they barely smolder, and the mountain ahead feels impossible to climb. That's the moment to dig deep—not into your own strength, but into the character of God.

He is the God who is worthy of our perseverance through trials and seasons of uncertainty. The God whose plans far exceed our understanding. Why press on? Because He desires a heart that is aligned with His purposes, not our own. Truthfully, you never know what He's preparing for His greater glory and your ultimate good.

My once-fired-up faith was muted and muffled. Hard circumstances have a way of doing that, don't they?

What I didn't tell you about that moment was that I had just changed jobs before the move. I was waist-deep in a PhD program. During the past twenty-four months, we had lost three close family members, including a twenty-six-year-old cousin who was like a brother to me, who died in a tragic interstate car accident. I had four children at home, ages five, three, eighteen months, and six months. We recently had a massive financial crisis, and my sweet wife, Jennifer, had just been diagnosed with a suspicious thyroid nodule and was now facing surgery.

Now this! I was done. The jubilant fire of faith that marked much of my Christian journey was now a smoldering memory. Even as I write this, the pain of that moment is so real I still want to take a shower and wash that memory away. I remember the perspective of having absolutely no control. We felt the weight of weakness in our bodies and spirits. The power of circumstances was gone. My job at DTS was about to vanish—or so I imagined—as visions of my face splashed across the front page of the *Dallas Morning News* and in every post office in America right alongside my two newest "friends" loomed in my imagination.

But worse than that . . . my once-fired-up faith was muted and muffled.

Hard circumstances have a way of doing that, don't they? But even in the worst of them, God is faithful. He never lets us draw down to zero before He offers His grace to rekindle our hearts and reset our faith ablaze with vision. Vision that directs the heart toward humble service to Him. He did that to me in a unique way. And that's precisely what happened to Moses too. Remember him? Forty years after hightailing it to Midian, after decades in the desert—God spoke to him!

> *One day Moses was tending the flock of his father-in-law, Jethro, the priest of Midian. He led the flock far into the wilderness and came to Sinai, the mountain of God. There the angel of the LORD appeared to him in a blazing fire from the middle of a bush. Moses stared in amazement. Though the bush was engulfed in flames, it didn't burn up. "This is amazing," Moses said to himself. "Why isn't that bush burning up? I must go see it."*
>
> *When the LORD saw Moses coming to take a closer look, God called to him from the middle of the bush, "Moses! Moses!"*
>
> *"Here I am," Moses replied.*
>
> *"Do not come any closer," the LORD warned. "Take off your sandals, for you are standing on holy ground. I am the God of your father—the God of Abraham, the God of Isaac, and the God of Jacob." When Moses heard this, he covered his face because he was afraid to look at God.* (EX. 3:1–6)

In a day, no, in a moment, God intervened in Moses' desert of faith and rekindled his heart with a vision for excellence, for holy purposes. Purposes greater than Moses. Purposes for God's greater plan. Character building purposes. For it is Him who we serve, not ourselves. Can you imagine what it must have felt like for Moses, disillusioned, exiled, and likely convinced his story was over, to hear the voice of God calling his name and casting a brand-new vision for his life? That's what God does when He steps in to fan the flame of weakened faith. He stokes the embers until they burn with bold trust again, calling us to serve Him with the very best of our heart and effort.

I'm convinced God still does this for each of us. The problem isn't His silence—it's often our unwillingness to notice. Sometimes, we simply refuse to see the burning bush right in front of us. But still, He calls. He beckons us—again and again—to rekindle our faith, to return to Him, and to step into the purpose He's been preparing all along.

Can renewing a commitment to wholeheartedly serve Jesus and others revive our walk with the Lord? Yes—it absolutely can. When we shift our focus from self to service, something changes inside us. We realign our hearts with Jesus' own mission: to love, to serve, to give, and to glorify the Father. Serving with all we have is more than just action—it's an act of worship, an expression of love, and a declaration of faith. It breathes life into weary hearts and redirects our attention and glorification to the One who first served us.

When we pour ourselves into others, we find that God is filling us with His Spirit. In giving, we're renewed. In surrender, we're strengthened. In serving Jesus with all that we have and are, we discover the revival our hearts have been longing for all along.

HALL OF REKINDLED HEARTS

Most of the people listed in Hebrews 11—the well-known "Hall of Faith"—didn't start out with unwavering, blazing trust in God. In fact, many of them stumbled, doubted, and struggled through long seasons of uncertainty. However, something shifted. At some point, their lives intersected with a moment of decision, a divine encounter, or a change in circumstance that rekindled their faith. What followed was a renewed commitment—an awakened trust that brought their once-smoldering belief back to life. And from that place of renewal, they reprioritized a humble service to God. It will be no longer from a sense of obligation, but instead from a heart of love, honor, and devotion to God.

A brief review of this hallmark passage (Heb. 11) will show how broadly God used so many different people, despite their self-focus and often difficult circumstances, to demonstrate His glory.

From Dysfunction to Devotion . . . Abel's Story

> *Faith shows the reality of what we hope for; it is the evidence of things we cannot see. Through their faith, the people in the days of old earned a good reputation.*
>
> *By faith we understand that the entire universe was formed at God's command, that what we now see did not come from anything that can be seen.*
>
> *It was by faith that Abel brought a more acceptable offering to God than Cain did. Abel's offering gave evidence that he was a righteous man, and God showed his approval of his gifts. Although Abel is long dead, he still speaks to us by his example of faith.* (HEB. 11:1–4)

Many of us understand the challenges that come with dysfunctional families—whether we've experienced it firsthand or witnessed the pain it causes in those close to us. The hurt and brokenness can often feel paralyzing. Sadly, the very first family, post-Genesis 3, displayed the heartache of jealousy and sinful self-serving motives. In Cain's situation, he succumbed to sin and killed his brother Abel in a fit of envy. It was Abel's faith the world remembers. Despite his tumultuous relationship with his brother, he trusted God and devoted himself to Him. His faith is recorded in history as a model for all who believe. He trusted in God to the very end.

It's so easy to give up on our faith, especially when we struggle to feel loved and accepted in our own family. So many kids, teenagers, young adults, and grown adults battle painful memories of a dysfunctional home life that douses the passion of their trust in God. You can easily allow that lingering pain or shame to cause you to fence yourself off from God's goodness. Your ears become dull to His loving voice. The flame of faith starts to flicker and dim. For some, it completely fades.

The good news is that God, in His kindness, never stops pursuing us.

The good news is that God, in His kindness, never stops pursuing us—just as He did with Moses. He meets us in the wilderness of hardship, right in the middle of our confusion, exhaustion, or disillusionment. And often, He uses those very circumstances to draw our hearts back to Him. Sometimes it's the loving persistence of a friend who gently invites us back into deeper relationship with the Lord. Other times, it's a quiet moment of conviction or a painful wake-up call that shifts our perspective. In those moments, God rekindles our faith—not by pushing us harder, but by turning our focus away from ourselves and back to Him. He calls us to serve with humility, to live for His glory, and to rediscover the joy of walking closely with Him.

Abel's experience, on the surface, was marked by tragedy. His story is one of deep pain and dysfunction—rooted in a sin-stained family dynamic. Yet, beneath the heartbreak, his unwavering faith in God stands as a timeless testimony. Abel's faith was costly. But it was also enduring. So enduring, in fact, that Scripture says of him: "Although Abel is long dead, he still speaks to us" (Heb. 11:4). Wow! That's the kind of faith that leaves a legacy. A faith that, even in the face of loss, stays the course and gives God everything. Abel didn't hold back—and his story continues to echo through history as a standard of wholehearted commitment to God.

From Sullenness to Surrender . . . Sarah's Story

Two people listed in Hebrews 11 are Abraham and Sarah. Let's face it, Abraham gets all the good press in the Bible. Rightly so, I suppose. Abraham, the father of faith, towers over most as one who willingly trusted the Lord through good times and bad to lead a nation and establish a pattern of faithfulness for all.

However, when the Holy Spirit inspired the author of the New Testament to pen the chapter on faith's champions, Sarah, Abraham's wife, made the list following him. What a tremendous joy to reflect on how God rekindled a dying ember of faith in one who would shine brightly to generations of women and men who struggle to believe against all odds.

A fading ember of faith: Sarah's story begins as her husband receives a remarkable message about her future with the Lord.

> *The Lord appeared again to Abraham near the oak grove belonging to Mamre. One day Abraham was sitting at the entrance to his tent during the hottest part of the day. He looked up and noticed three men standing nearby. When he saw them, he ran to meet them and welcomed them, bowing low to the ground.*

"My lord," he said, "if it pleases you, stop here for a while. Rest in the shade of this tree while water is brought to wash your feet. And since you've honored your servant with this visit, let me prepare some food to refresh you before you continue on your journey."

"All right," they said. "Do as you have said." . . .

"Where is Sarah, your wife?" the visitors asked. "She's inside the tent," Abraham replied. Then one of them said, "I will return to you about this time next year, and your wife, Sarah, will have a son!"

Sarah was listening to this conversation from the tent. Abraham and Sarah were both very old by this time, and Sarah was long past the age of having children. So she laughed silently to herself and said, "How could a worn-out woman like me enjoy such pleasure, especially when my master—my husband—is also so old?"

Then the LORD said to Abraham, "Why did Sarah laugh? Why did she say, 'Can an old woman like me have a baby?' Is anything too hard for the LORD? I will return about this time next year, and Sarah will have a son." (GEN. 18:1–4, 9–14)

Go back and reread that story. Sense the jadedness of Sarah's struggling faith. After a lifetime of facing the shame (in her culture and her perceived value) and sorrow of never knowing the joy of a child's laughter in her home and cowering under the relentless dishonor of being barren, she struggled to believe God's voice. It made her laugh.

The decades of bitter struggle to understand God's purpose

in her pain must have battered her flickering faith like the relentless sand and heat of her wilderness surroundings.

A Rekindled Faith in the Wilderness

That faith had totally diminished when God's messengers of grace appeared to Abraham that day. Somewhere in the long white space of biblical time . . . down through the pages of God's mysterious ways, Sarah's faith rekindled. She bore a son, she raised him in faith, she witnessed the wonder of the Lord's eternal power and purpose, and her faith blazed across time as generations of believers to come would celebrate God's epitaph for Sarah . . .

> *It was by faith that even Sarah was able to have a child, though she was barren and was too old. She believed that God would keep his promise. And so a whole nation came from this one man who was as good as dead—a nation with so many people that, like the stars in the sky and the sand on the seashore, there is no way to count them.* (HEB. 11:11–12)

A flickering faith can be rekindled even in the bleakest array of circumstances. Sarah's story bears a vibrant witness to that truth. It may be part of your story as you read this chapter. Perhaps it's why a loving friend or family member gave you this book. I want to urge you, friend, whatever the cause of your sullen trust at this juncture of your journey with God, you can experience a renewed rekindling of your faith in Him. He is tender and gracious to all who turn to Him to restore trust and know His power. And He frequently draws us to Him in our darkest moments.

My wife, Jennifer, has a story to tell—one born out of deep struggle. After the birth of our third child, Jennifer's system began to crash. There's no doubt it was physiological at its core, but over time, things went from bad to worse. Her energy was depleted, and her perspective dimmed. She was crashing, and we both knew it. Like so many in similar situations, we went from doctor to doctor, searching for help. But answers were hard to come by. Eventually, the label "postpartum depression" was offered—a catch-all diagnosis for what she was experiencing. Medication was prescribed to help manage the symptoms, and while it brought some relief, it didn't touch the deeper issue. Something else was unraveling beneath the surface—her spiritual state. Her faith, once strong and steady, began to shake. She wrestled with fear and anxiety in ways neither of us had ever experienced before. Honestly, it frightened me. The confident, vibrant woman I once knew seemed to slip away, replaced by someone distant, quiet, and withdrawn. There were days when I spoke to her, and I wasn't sure who I was talking to anymore.

God frequently uses pain to force us to face Him. When we do, He will ignite our dormant faith embers and turn them into a furious flame for His glory.

I'll admit to something difficult to confess—I made it worse. Not out of neglect, but out of desperation. I did what many of us "fixers" do—I tried to solve the problem. If you're a fixer, you know exactly what I mean. We rush in with solutions, strategies, and action steps. But what she really needed wasn't a fix. She needed presence. She needed someone to listen—truly listen—and simply to be there.

Yet God was gracious. Over time, and through the counsel of friends, and more importantly, through immersion in God's Word, Jennifer learned to submit that fear to the Lord and stand confidently in His power. And so did I. Ultimately, what both of us realized was that it was a spiritual battle as well. Oh, the physical ramifications were real and metabolic, for sure, but we believe the evil one used it to rattle our spiritual fervor. We also believe that God used that moment to help us trust in new ways that strengthened our trust in Him and each other. I know this: God frequently uses pain to force us to face Him. When we do, He will ignite our dormant faith embers and turn them into a furious flame for His glory. On the backside of that re-committed reality is power—humble power, but a revived faith full of vigor and purpose in a Sovereign God.

THE CALL TO A RENEWED COMMITMENT

Faith in Christ is not a one-time experience but a lifelong journey of deepening devotion and service. Life takes its toll. So does sin. So does discouragement and at times the sheer monotony of day after day following God, raising kids, and slugging it out at work, often without recognition or advancement. Life pushes hard against a vibrant faith. Sometimes it burns to a flicker. We've all been there. I get it. Just as a warm campfire can begin to die out if left unattended, so too can our faith if not *intentionally nurtured.* Rekindling our faith in Christ requires a renewed commitment to serving Him in every aspect of life—our work, our relationships, and our personal growth.

I wonder if that's what the apostle Paul had in mind when he wrote to young Timothy to bolster his commitment to the Lord.

> *I remember your genuine faith, for you share the faith that first filled your grandmother Lois and your mother, Eunice. And I know that same faith continues strong in you. This is why I remind you to fan into flames the spiritual gift God*

> *gave you when I laid my hands on you. For God has not given us a spirit of fear and timidity, but of power, love, and self-discipline.* (2 TIM. 1:5–7)

Even though Timothy enjoyed a strong legacy of faith that had originated with his grandmother, perhaps life and the tricky matter of serving a fledgling church had begun to douse his spiritual passion. He needed a reminder to do his part to rekindle his faith and to fan the flame of his love to serve the Lord. If you visit ancient Ephesus today, you will see its city structure in ruins. However, the legacy of faith nurtured by Timothy's powerful and passionate ministry to that impressive church in Ephesus lives on. Can you imagine your Christian life without the New Testament book of Ephesians?

A REKINDLED PURPOSE IN SERVING CHRIST IN ALL THAT WE DO

Timothy's story reminds me of another Bible passage where Paul offers a similar reminder to believers struggling against the pressure of persecution and the difficulties that life brings.

Paul wrote,

> *Serve them sincerely because of your reverent fear of the Lord. Work willingly at whatever you do, as though you were working for the Lord rather than for people. Remember that the Lord will give you an inheritance as your reward, and that the Master you are serving is Christ.* (COL. 3:22B–24)

Colossians 3:23–24 reminds us that our work and service should be carried out as unto the Lord, not merely for human approval. Our faith flame can be rekindled even brighter by remembering the Lord rewards us for faithful service for Christ. How easy is it to become discouraged by the fickle response of a difficult employer or stingy company that fails to reward hard work appropriately!

However, even in the doldrums of life, when our focus shifts to the joy of receiving a reward from Christ Himself—our Master—the flame of faith can burn brightly once again. His perspective transforms the mundane into moments of worship and elevates everyday responsibilities into divine callings.

Many believers experience spiritual stagnation because they compartmentalize their faith—separating it from the routine of daily life. Paul reminds us in Colossians 3 that *whatever we do*—whether in ministry, our career, or within our families—should be done as service to Christ.

When we realign our perspective and see our daily tasks as sacred opportunities to glorify Him, faith blazes. The ordinary becomes extraordinary. And the slow, steady burn of obedience becomes a fire that lights the way for others.

Faith Expressed Through Work

Jesus often used work-related parables to teach kingdom principles. One such example is found in Matthew 25:14–30. It was a story of a man who left on a trip, but before he embarked, he entrusted a certain amount of money to a few of his servants. He wanted them to be wise stewards of that investment while he was away, hoping they would use their time and talents well. Two servants did well and doubled the amount while the boss was gone. The third servant, however, was afraid of losing the bag of money and buried it in the ground. When the master returned, he found, to his joy, that two of his servants had done well, worked hard, and realized a healthy return on his investment. The other, sadly, had faltered. He had missed the opportunity to please his master.

As believers in Christ, we have received an incredible opportunity to serve Him and return to Him a lifetime of valuable ministry. As Romans 12:1 (NIV) says, we can offer our bodies "as a living sacrifice, holy and pleasing to God." Unfortunately, we too, sometimes falter and allow fear, the vice-grip of discouragement, or adversity to quell our initial passion. Yet, that faith can be rekindled by returning to our first love for Christ—a renewed passion for serving Him . . . for His glory . . . not ours.

The Bible contains examples of individuals who glorified God through their work. Joseph, for instance, served diligently in Potiphar's house and later in Pharaoh's court (Gen. 39–41). His commitment to excellence in his various situations demonstrated his faithfulness to God. Daniel exemplified an unwavering commitment to God as an administrator in Babylon, refusing to compromise his faith while excelling in his duties (Dan. 6:3–5).

When we begin to see our work as an extension of our faith, everything changes. We shift our mindset from viewing tasks as mere obligations to embracing them as opportunities to glorify God. That perspective ignites a renewed passion in our daily responsibilities and deepens our spiritual connection with Christ. Suddenly, we're not just checking off to-do lists—we're stepping into sacred moments. Our eyes are opened to opportunities given to us by the Lord—moments where He desires to teach us, shape us, and draw us closer through the privilege of serving others. When service is seen through the lens of worship, even the ordinary becomes holy.

Faith in Relationships

Serving the Lord extends beyond our work, including our relationships. Paul writes, "Don't be selfish; don't try to impress others. Be humble, thinking of others as better than yourselves" (Phil. 2:3). Whether in marriage, friendships, or community service, when we serve others as worship, we reflect the heart of Christ and experience renewed faith. Faith is rekindled by a renewed commitment to serve others, not ourselves.

Jesus emphasized love and service in relationships as well.

> *"This is my commandment: Love each other in the same way I have loved you. There is no greater love than to lay down one's life for one's friends."* (JOHN 15:12–13)

When we cultivate Christlike love in our relationships, we foster deeper connections and rekindle our faith. Loving others, especially those closest to us, significantly reduces the temptation to harbor bitterness when we are wronged. Few things douse the passion of our faith like an unforgiving spirit. Again, Paul captured this principle in his letter to the Colossians.

> *Make allowance for each other's faults, and forgive anyone who offends you. Remember, the Lord forgave you, so you must forgive others."* (COL. 3:13)

We maintain a vibrant faith by fostering a spirit of forgiveness and grace in relationships. Practicing forgiveness restores relationships and rekindles our faith by aligning our hearts with Christ's example.

Service in the Community

A renewed faith often takes root through selfless service. When we step into acts of kindness, we tap into the joy of Christ's love in action. As Acts 20:35 reminds us: "You should remember the words of the Lord Jesus: 'It is more blessed to give than to receive.'" Whether it's volunteering at a shelter, mentoring a young believer, helping an overwhelmed young mother, or simply spending time with a lonely neighbor—these seemingly small acts carry eternal weight. They enhance our faith by reconnecting us with Christ's call to serve. Jesus said, "Wake up and look around. The fields are already ripe for harvest" (John 4:35). In other words, the opportunities are already in front of us. We don't have to search far to be of service to the King. What we need are eyes that see and a heart that's willing. When that's our posture, renewed faith is never far behind.

BREAKING FREE FROM LUKEWARM CHRISTIANITY

In Revelation 3:15–16, Jesus warns against lukewarm faith. He lamented the fact that believers were neither hot nor cold. A stagnant faith results from a lack of passionate pursuit of God's calling. To rekindle our faith, we must reject complacency. He is calling us to unapologetically serve Him.

Now, the rest of the story from earlier in this chapter. Remember when my hands were up against the wall with my two new friends? I didn't realize that the Lord was addressing my pity party and bringing me out of my spiritual slumber. He called me into service, but I didn't realize it at the time. He was blowing on my dormant embers of faith and asking me to wake up. Here is what happened:

The police officer cuffed the two women who stood on each side of me. He knew who they were; they'd had some type of run-in before. But he did not cuff me. One officer said something about seeing a "smoking truck" on the highway in front of Uncle Hermon's Club, and they were wondering if my story was on the up-and-up.

After marching all three of us out, he put the women in the back of the police car. He then looked at me, then turned and looked at the truck. He looked at me carefully and said,

"Slowly put your hand in your pocket and take out whatever you need to show me." I remember pausing, heart pounding, and asking, "Are you sure it's okay for me to reach in and pull out the receipt?" He laughed and said, "Show me what you got." I pulled out the key and truck receipt and pointed to the broken truck that (thankfully) still had a trickle of smoke coming out of the engine. There was a long pause. Looking at me, the car, and then his partner, he said, "I guess you're legit." He got in his car and drove off.

My dad drives up thirty seconds later to pick me up, finding me standing there white as a ghost and still in shock. Rolling down the window, he said, "What's the matter with you? Get in the car. We're going to be late." At that point, I think I started mumbling again. I said, "Dad, you won't believe this even if I tell you." When we finally made it to church for our meeting, all the other leaders laughed at my expense. And, of course, I stayed up till four in the morning, leaving messages with the truck rental company—reporting that my truck had blown up on the side of the road. I documented where it was. It was an ordeal I finally was happy to have behind me. Or so I thought.

Two days later, I was in my office on campus when the phone rang. It was an officer from our police department on campus. He said that he had talked with one of his friends at the Dallas Police Department and that there was a warrant out for my arrest because of a stolen vehicle from the truck rental center. I couldn't believe it! As I talked to the campus police chief, he convinced his friend to hold off after he explained to him what had happened. They agreed to wait forty-eight hours to see if I could resolve the matter.

As you can imagine, I immediately contacted the truck rental center and explained the situation. After working through management, we eventually found out that I had done everything right in reporting the blown-up truck, but that the night manager had not reported it on his end; hence the perspective of the stolen truck.

Knowing it was their error, they apologized for the mistake of their employee and said they would waive all the truck rental fees. I must admit—I thought, *Waive the fees? That's it? I'm thinking, dude—I want a trip to Tahiti out of this thing for all my pain and suffering!* But they did waive all my fees, and I was thankful for that. As we talked, they said, "One more thing. We're going to send you a complaint form. We need you to document all this, and when we receive it—we assure you that the night manager who messed up will be terminated immediately." I remember thinking *I don't want this guy to lose his job . . . I . . . I just want a trip to Tahiti!* So, I told them to keep their form and work on job improvement. Finally, with that call, the saga was over. Or so I thought.

Start serving—it's one of God's tools to fan the flame of faith!

The next day, I was in my office, and the phone rang. On the other end, I heard, "Uh, Mr. Yarbrough?" He continued, "I'm the night manager at the truck rental center, and I want to apologize to you. I dropped the ball, and because of that, you ended up in a really difficult situation with the police. I'm so sorry for the inconvenience and stress that I caused you. Sir, thank you for not filling out that complaint form. If you had done that, I'd have lost my job, and I don't know what we would have done."

I was stunned. He then said the words I will never forget. "Thank you for not getting me fired. My wife and I are having lots of problems right now and . . . my wife was just diagnosed with cancer . . . and I don't know what we're going to do." Do you remember my story? Jennifer's thyroid cancer? This could *not* be a coincidence. It hit me like a two-by-four across the head. By God's sovereign design—and amid my pain—God had opened wide a moment for His glory, and He was asking me to enlist in His service to help someone else.

That night, I had the privilege of going down to the truck rental center, sharing the gospel with the night manager and his wife, and watching them come to faith. God asked me to serve through the pain and to remember what matters. Through that service, He rekindled my heart and revived my faith. He wants to do that with you too. Start serving, friends. It's one of God's tools to fan the flame of faith!

SERVICE AS A SPIRITUAL DISCIPLINE

Just as athletes must continuously train to hone their skills for better performance, we must actively seek to grow through prayer, by studying and applying God's Word, and by serving others. Paul wrote to Timothy:

> *Work hard so you can present yourself to God and receive his approval. Be a good worker, one who does not need to be ashamed and who correctly explains the word of truth.* (2 TIM. 2:15)

> It is not about perfection. It's about giving our hearts and lives to God as a testimony of His grace. It's for His glory. Consider this:

> *So whether you eat or drink, or whatever you do, do it all for the glory of God.* (1 COR. 10:31)

Developing service habits draws us closer to Christ and fuels the flame of our faith. Striving to model a life of service requires intentionality too. That might mean setting goals for how to serve and where to serve. It may mean assessing your spiritual gifts with a pastor or spiritual mentor. It could also mean recommitting to prayer daily and seeking guidance from the Lord. The psalmist declared: "The teaching of your word gives light, so even the simple can understand" (Ps. 119:130).

Who doesn't need light and understanding to guide us in everything—including a heart of service? Actively serving in ministry and seeking accountability from fellow believers also keeps faith alive. Remember Solomon's words: "As iron sharpens iron, so a friend sharpens a friend" (Prov. 27:17).

Surrounding ourselves with like-minded believers who encourage and challenge us is vital for rekindling our faith.

A RENEWED COMMITMENT TO CHRIST

Rekindling our faith begins with a renewed commitment to serving the Lord with excellence—with all we've got, in every area of life. I know life can be hard. In certain seasons, it can feel almost unbearable. So I want to be careful not to offer empty platitudes here—especially if you're facing one of those impossible scenarios. What I *do* want to offer you is hope, and also a gentle challenge.

No matter what you're walking through, Jesus desires to reveal Himself to you. He wants to show you His power, His grace, and His goodness. He wants to rekindle your confidence in His purposes and plans for your life, even when they don't make sense or even when they hurt.

He longs to bring something new into your story, to reignite your faith in His power, His love, His kindness, and His heart for *you.* Sometimes, He even nudges us to serve *while* we're still hurting. And somehow, mysteriously and beautifully, that act of service becomes the very fuel He uses to reignite the fire within us.

So, I'm going to pause in this moment and pray for you—yes, right now. I'm asking God to transcend time and space to meet you right where you are, in whatever need or pain you carry.

Trust Him. He is faithful.

And He is worth serving.

MORE KINDLING . . .

1. How did the Lord speak to you in this chapter? What specific insight did you receive from Him?
2. How can you rekindle your faith by renewing your willingness to serve Him? What might be blocking you from moving forward with that?
3. Who in your life (list some names) might be willing to join you in helping you work through some challenges to your ability to serve Christ joyfully and in freedom?

5

REKINDLED SERVANTHOOD

Genuine Humility

Clothe yourselves with humility toward one another.

1 PETER 5:5 NIV

The fifth essential for rekindling the joy of our faith is like the last, but in many ways, it stands alone as it envisions a new and transformed mindset about how you live your life before the Lord and others. I'm talking about what I call *genuine humility*—pursuing authentic selflessness. It's a requisite for all who walk with the Lord.

I will never forget hearing about a group of kids who decided to build a clubhouse. They all wanted to pitch in and participate, but their diverse backgrounds and personalities soon erupted into conflict and chaos. Progress on the much-anticipated clubhouse ground to a halt. Finally, one of the kids had a flash of insight. "We need some easy rules for the clubhouse so we can all get along!"

So, they came up with three simple rules:

RULE #1: NOBODY ACT BIG
RULE #2: NOBODY ACT LITTLE
RULE #3: EVERYBODY ACT MEDIUM

Isn't that great? Genuine humility means acting *medium.* That simply means we don't act big, which is the purest form of pride. It means always advancing our own agenda at the expense of everyone else. Acting little is a false sense of humility, which still demands attention to self by feigning need or looking for sympathy.

Acting *medium* looks like Jesus. We should take the humble position and make sure that we view ourselves rightly before God and others. To rekindle the joy of our faith, we must come to terms with the reality that God is sovereign and we are not. The Bible is full of stories of individuals just like you and me who, at times and in various ways, came to that conclusion.

HUMBLE HEROES: STORIES OF OBEDIENT FAITH AND GOD'S BLESSING

Throughout Scripture, a golden thread weaves together the stories of men and women who humbly obeyed God—even when it didn't seem to make sense—and found themselves wrapped in His blessings. Their lives remind us that faith is not about having all the answers; it's about trusting the One who does. Let's step into the sandals of some of these humble heroes.

Abraham: The Man Who Walked Without a Map

Abraham, once called Abram, led a nomadic life. Successful it seems, he had drawn the attention of the Lord as the one designated to start a people who would one day be set apart for God's glorious purposes. Considered the father of faith, his life took a dramatic turn as he came face-to-face with the sovereign God of heaven.

> *One day Terah took his son Abram, his daughter-in-law Sarai (his son Abram's wife), and his grandson Lot (his son Haran's child) and moved away from Ur of the Chaldeans. He was headed for the land of Canaan, but they stopped at Haran and settled there. Terah lived for 205 years and died while still in Haran.*
>
> *The LORD had said to Abram, "Leave your native country, your relatives, and your father's family, and go to the land that I will show you. I will make you into a great nation. I will bless you and make you famous, and you will be a blessing to others. I will bless those who bless you and curse those who treat you with contempt. All the families of earth will be blessed through you."* (GEN. 11:31—12:3)

Imagine packing your whole family and everything you own, leaving the comfort of family and home, and embarking to a place that was not yet confirmed. No forwarding address, no sense of the climate or culture to which you would go.

What a remarkable thing. But Abraham did just that. That monumental trust in God required a genuine humility—a selflessness that compelled Abraham to change his life's course completely. It meant the possible surrender of future wealth from a growing livestock operation, and upending his family to submit to God's sovereign will. Oh, I assure you that he didn't do everything correctly. God told him to leave his people—and he took Lot. Don't miss it—Lot was one of his peeps! That caused him great grief down the road. But give props to

Abram. At least he went. Would you have gone? Would you have headed off into the unknown? Well, Abram did!

That move of humble faith sparked a flame of trust and faithfulness that would burn brightly for countless generations to come and ultimately become God's gift of grace through which Christ the Messiah would warm the hearts of sinners from every nation on earth. Remember—Jesus is Jewish, and thus came through the line of Abram (Matt. 1:1).

I remember one of my visits to Israel and the much-anticipated stop at Jerusalem. As the crowd pressed to enter the Sheep's Gate, there were a dozen or so Arab boys selling beautifully colored garments, beaded belts, and sandals. One of them smiled brightly at me and said, "Good morning! Welcome to Jerusalem, the capital of the world!"

I remember thinking, *That kid is right! The whole world has come to this place . . . Arabs, Gentiles, Europeans, Persians, Asians, and every tribe and nation to express a trust in God, a faith in the One He sent, and the One who came from the faith of Abraham.* So much flowed from that profound step of humble faith by a man who believed God and set out with no clue to where he was going.

Have you ever taken a bold step of humble faith, one that you couldn't fully understand, but you knew the Lord was leading you to do so? I have. That step of faith landed me at DTS.

After having been a student in the early 1990s, I served at my undergraduate alma mater, Dallas Christian College (DCC). Over a five-year window, I taught in the Bible department—eventually serving as vice president. Those were wonderful years.

Somehow along the way, DTS was in a leadership transition. Dr. Charles "Chuck" Swindoll was moving from president to chancellor, and Dr. Mark Bailey had been invited by the DTS board to serve as president. Much to my surprise, Dr. Bailey invited me to leave my post at DCC and serve as his research assistant. Along with such duties, I would also serve Dr. Swindoll. The opportunity tugged at my heart. I loved my role at the college. But serving alongside and assisting Drs. Bailey and Swindoll—what an opportunity. What to do?

After much prayer and consultation from trusted advisors, Jennifer and I clearly felt the Lord leading us to DTS in terms of employment ministry. Then I found out something that challenged our perspective—the change would come with a significant pay cut! Yikes. It was a scary decision, but the Lord impressed on us that was what we were to do, so we did it. Little did we know the Lord had plans that we could not see. He simply asked us to trust Him and go in humility and dependence. In a position of dependence. Forced to trust Him as we went. It's not always a pleasant position to be in, but it's a position that builds faith.

> *It was by faith that Abraham obeyed when God called him to leave home and go to another land that God would give him as his inheritance. He went without knowing where he was going.* (HEB. 11:8)

When asked by God to leave his home and way of life without knowing what was ahead, Abraham did it. When God told him, "Go to the land that I will show you" (Gen. 12:1), Abraham packed up and left.

His humble obedience wasn't a one-time thing, either. When asked to sacrifice his son Isaac—the very son through whom God promised to bless the nations—Abraham obeyed again (Gen. 22:1–18). His faith didn't demand full understanding. He simply trusted God's goodness. Read the story of Abraham carefully, and you will find that his faith wavered on occasions. He has moments of great failure, as we all do. However, he believed and trusted God to direct his steps. By the grace of God, the Lord blessed him beyond imagination: "And through your descendants all the nations of the earth will be blessed—all because you have obeyed me" (Gen. 22:18). We are part of that blessing today!

Moses: The Reluctant Leader with a Willing Heart

> *Now the man Moses was very humble, more humble than any other person on earth.* (NUM. 12:3)

As we saw in the last chapter, Moses didn't exactly sprint into spiritual greatness. When God called him from the burning bush (Ex. 3–4), Moses hesitated, listing all the reasons he wasn't qualified. His faith at one point was but an ember! Yet despite his fears and weaknesses, Moses ultimately submitted to God's call with a humble heart.

In leading the Israelites out of Egypt, receiving the Ten Commandments, and interceding for a rebellious people, Moses became a powerful example of humble, faith-filled obedience. He wasn't perfect—he had moments of frustration and failure—but his heart kept turning back to God. Because Moses trusted and obeyed, he saw God's glory in ways few others have. He was privileged to witness from the crevice of a rock the glory of God pass by (Ex. 33:20–23).

Ruth: The Faithful Foreigner Who Found Favor

Ruth was a Moabite, a foreigner who had no obligation to stay loyal to her Israelite mother-in-law, Naomi, after her husband died. Yet out of love and humble faith, Ruth chose to follow Naomi—and, more importantly, Naomi's God. When Naomi encouraged her to return to her family,

> *Ruth replied, "Don't ask me to leave you and turn back. Wherever you go, I will go; wherever you live, I will live. Your people will be my people, and your God will be my God."* (RUTH 1:16)

She didn't know what the future held. She didn't make grand speeches. She simply did the next right thing, gleaning in the fields to provide for herself and Naomi (Ruth 2:2–3). Through her humble obedience and trust, Ruth lit a flame of faith that ultimately led to her becoming the great-grandmother of King David, from whose covenant lineage came Jesus Christ Himself (Matt. 1:1, 5–6).

David: The Shepherd King After God's Heart

> *Then Samuel said to Jesse, "Are all your sons here?" And he said, "There remains yet the youngest, but behold, he is keeping the sheep."* (1 SAM. 16:11 ESV)

When Samuel came to anoint Israel's next king, David wasn't even invited to the lineup. He was out with the sheep—serving faithfully in obscurity. However, God saw his heart: "The LORD doesn't see things the way you see them. People judge by outward appearance, but the LORD looks at the heart" (1 SAM. 16:7).

David's life was marked by humble obedience, from facing Goliath with a sling and five stones (1 Sam. 17) to patiently waiting years to take the throne God promised him. He even refused to harm King Saul when given the opportunity (1 Sam. 24:6), when getting Saul out of the way might have hastened his ascension to the kingship.

Despite his serious sins later in life, David learned the rich reward of returning to God with a broken and contrite heart (Ps. 51). His life overflowed with the blessings of God's promises, including the everlasting covenant that the Messiah would come through his line (2 Sam. 7:16).

Mary: The Young Woman Who Said "Yes"

> *And Mary said, "Behold, I am the servant of the Lord; let it be to me according to your word."* (LUKE 1:38 ESV)

When the angel Gabriel announced to a teenage girl that she would carry the Son of God, Mary could have said no. After all, accepting would mean risking her reputation, her future marriage to Joseph, and possibly even her life.

Yet her response was breathtaking in its simplicity and humility: "I am the servant of the Lord." She trusted God fully, even in the mystery. Hers was one of the most stunning examples of selflessness and humility in all of Scripture.

Because Mary said yes, she experienced the greatest blessing imaginable: birthing the Savior of the world and watching God's promises spark a flame of trust that would last a lifetime (Luke 1:45–49) and an eternity (John 3:16).

Peter: The Bold Fisherman Who Learned Humble Faith

> *Simon Peter replied, "Lord, to whom would we go? You have the words that give eternal life."* (JOHN 6:68)

By all accounts, Peter wasn't naturally humble. He was often bold and brash. On many occasions, he stuck his foot in his mouth, and sometimes his whole leg! Yet through his relationship with Jesus, Peter learned the power of humble obedience.

He left everything to follow Jesus (Luke 5:10–11). He stepped out of the boat to walk on water (Matt. 14:29). He stumbled, denying three times that he even knew Jesus (Luke 22:61–62)—but after the resurrection, he humbly received Jesus' forgiveness and commission to "feed my sheep" (John 21:17). We'll revisit that story later.

One thing is for sure: Peter's story is one of transformation. His faith grew into a bold but humble leadership that helped launch the early church (Acts 2). God blessed Peter's obedience with a legacy that still inspires Christians today.

Paul: The Relentless Missionary with a Surrendered Heart

> *"But my life is worth nothing to me unless I use it for finishing the work assigned me by the Lord Jesus."*
> (ACTS 20:24)

Once a fierce persecutor of Christians, Paul's encounter with the risen Jesus on the road to Damascus (Acts 9) turned his world upside down. His pride was shattered. His plans were surrendered. A Jew's Jew, a Hebrew of Hebrews, Paul had the pedigree to rise in the ranks of Judaism. However, God had other plans for him. After his encounter with Christ, Paul devoted the rest of his life to preaching the gospel no matter the cost—beatings, shipwrecks, imprisonments, and eventually martyrdom. Because Paul humbly obeyed God's call, the gospel spread across the Roman world, and at least thirteen[1] New Testament books come from his Spirit-inspired letters. His life shines with the blessings of a race faithfully run (2 Tim. 4:7–8).

WALKING IN THEIR FOOTSTEPS

Each of these stories reminds us that God's blessings aren't reserved for the flawless or the fearless. They are best reserved for the humble-hearted—those willing to trust Him, even when it's hard. Their journeys encourage us today. When we choose faith over fear, obedience over comfort, God meets us with His powerful, surprising, life-changing blessings.

THE JOY OF A LOW PLACE

This joy-giving paradox in the Christian life can only be discovered by living it. The lower we bow before Christ and others, the higher our joy ascends. By letting go of the need to promote ourselves, we open the door for the Holy Spirit to rekindle the joy of our faith. In a world addicted to status, power, and platform, humility feels foreign, even foolish. The allure of the spotlight on stage can suck you in and convince you that you are "all-that." It preys on our quest for attention and affirmation. Yet Scripture reveals that the way up in the kingdom is always down. This is not mere pious theory—it's the lived pattern of our Lord and the unshakable pathway to rekindled joy.

Paul's letter to the Philippians is saturated with joy, yet it was penned from a prison cell. Central to its message is the humility of Jesus, the servant-King who emptied Himself. For those longing to bring the fire back to their faith, this letter invites you to rediscover joy through Christlike humility, lived out in sacrificial service. The words of a chorus I grew up singing are spot on: "If you want to be great in God's kingdom, learn to be the servant of all." It's not just a model. It's a mandate for followers of the King.

THE CALL TO HUMILITY: A CHRIST-CENTERED MANDATE

Paul begins Philippians 2 with a heart-plea to the church:

> *Is there any encouragement from belonging to Christ? Any comfort from his love? Any fellowship together in the Spirit? Are your hearts tender and compassionate?* (v. 1)

The apostle connects spiritual unity and joy with the cultivation of humility. For the Philippians—and for us—joy and humility are not separate virtues but interdependent. Without humility, unity fractures. Without unity, joy fades. Then he adds: "Don't be selfish; don't try to impress others. Be humble, thinking of others as better than yourselves" (v. 3). This is radical. It flies in the face of our default flesh-driven tendencies. The Christian life is cruciform—shaped by the cross. To follow Jesus means embracing downward mobility in a world chasing the climb. There is an obvious application for us as believers. We are asked to shift the focus from us to others; from us to Him. Humility requires a conscious transferal from self-centeredness to Christ-centeredness. Ask daily:

"Whose glory am I seeking—mine or Christ's?"

"Who is being lifted up in my conversations and choices?"

Genuine humility does not think less of oneself; it simply thinks of oneself less. It's the posture that opens the heart to God's joy.

CHRIST'S EXAMPLE: THE HUMILITY OF HEAVEN

The clearest image of humility in all of Scripture is found in Philippians 2:5–11. Paul exalts Christ as both model and motivation:

> *Though he was God, he did not think of equality with God as something to cling to.*
> *Instead, He gave up His divine privileges.* (vv. 6–7)

This descent of Christ—often called the *kenosis* or self-emptying—is the greatest act of humility in history, earthly or eternal. Jesus did not cease to be God, but He laid aside His rights, taking the form of a servant. First, he took on flesh. He became man. Can you imagine? The Creator (Col. 1) stepping into the mire and muck of this world. He came down to our level, because we couldn't come up to His.

Leaving His rightful position of authority, He positioned Himself as a servant, not royalty. On advent number one, He came as a frail baby in Bethlehem, whose first cries were heard by an outcast peasant girl and her betrothed husband. That act of humble obedience would lead this God-man to die on the cross for the sins of all mankind. Yes, the eternal Son came to wash dusty feet, embrace lepers, and carry a sinner's cross. Joy, for Jesus, was found in obedience and love—not in status or applause. Rest assured He garnered the applause of heaven, but this old, dark, sin-stained world rejected Him. Even more so, His own people did. As John said, "He came to his own people, and even they rejected him" (John 1:11).

REFLECTION: WHAT PRIVILEGES CAN YOU LAY DOWN?

The call to imitate Christ's humility is not theoretical. It challenges us to relinquish control, comfort, recognition, and entitlement for the sake of others. Ask yourself:

"What rights or privileges am I holding too tightly?"

"How can I use my position or resources to humbly serve others without recognition or notoriety?"

While Christ is our ultimate example, Scripture provides powerful portraits of humble disciples who lived authentic selflessness, leading to genuine joy. Note these characters and moments in the biblical text.

- John the Baptist: "He must become greater; I must become less" (John 3:30 NIV). John understood his role as a preparer of the way, not *the* Way. His joy was complete in seeing Christ exalted. Humility relinquishes the spotlight and willingly fades into the background, allowing the glory to go to Jesus alone.

- Mary of Bethany: Serving with Extravagant Love (John 12:1–8) Mary humbled herself at Jesus' feet, anointing Him with costly perfume. Her act, dismissed by others, was honored by Christ and revered by the faithful for generations to come. Humility doesn't calculate usefulness; it pours out everything in joyful worship of Christ.

- Paul the Apostle: Boasting Only in Weakness (2 Cor. 12:9) Paul, though brilliant and bold, embraced his weakness, which set the stage for God's strength to shine through him. His ministry was marked by vulnerability and service, not domination and applause.

HUMILITY REKINDLES JOY

The lie of the world is that self-promotion leads to fulfillment. Yet self-exaltation frequently breeds anxiety and loneliness. Genuine humility, however, reconnects us to the source of joy—Jesus Christ. Think of the benefits of humility:

Frees us from comparison

Enables unity in the church

Cultivates compassion for others

Anchors our identity in Christ

Releases us from the trap of performance

Liberates us from the quest for self-promotion and external validation

That's why Jesus said, "It is more blessed to give than to receive" (Acts 20:35). That word "blessed" carries the idea of deep, soul-rooted joy. In serving others, we express the joy Jesus offers.

THE PRACTICE OF HUMILITY: MAKING IT REAL

Humility must be practiced intentionally, not passively absorbed. Here are a few ways to cultivate it daily:

Confess pride regularly . . .

Humility begins with honest self-awareness. Pray David's prayer: "Search me, God. . . . See if there is any offensive way in me" (Ps. 139:23–24 NIV). Confession keeps our hearts tender.

Serve in hidden places . . .

Serve the Lord graciously and willingly without recognition. Pick up the unnoticed tasks. Jesus washed feet in secret before He was glorified. Joy often rises in obscurity.

Listen more than you speak . . .

James exhorts us to be "quick to listen, slow to speak" (James 1:19). Listening well honors others and silences pride.

Celebrate when others succeed . . .

Jealousy stifles joy. Rejoice when others are elevated. Humility is not threatened by someone else's blessing.

Practice submission to God and others . . .

Humility yields. It bows the knee to God's timing, leadership, and correction. "God opposes the proud but gives grace to the humble" (1 Peter 5:5).

SACRIFICIAL SERVICE: THE PATH TO LASTING IMPACT

Humility is not a mere attitude, although that is required. It also involves authentic action. Sacrificial service is humility wearing skin. It costs us something but yields eternal rewards.

Jesus said, "Whoever wants to be a leader among you must be your servant" (Matt. 20:26). Greatness in the kingdom is measured by towel-bearing, not title-holding. There are countless ways this could be applied in our walks of faith.

Mentor a younger believer without seeking recognition.

Serve in a ministry area outside your comfort zone, like playing games with special-needs children in the church or serving the homeless.

Forgive someone who wounded your pride and be the first to initiate reconciliation.

Assist someone financially—anonymously.

Mow the yard of a family in need when they are not home.

Send a note of encouragement to someone who needs a pick-me-up.

Need I go on? The opportunities for humble service are limitless in this broken and needy world. Here is the side benefit. When we serve in humility, the joy of faith is rekindled. Trust me, friend—sparks will fly and flames will burst forth. God's Holy Spirit fills what we empty. Joy ignites where selfish ambition once burned.

CHURCH CULTURE AND THE CRISIS OF PRIDE

The call to live in selfless service is not just an individual matter. Yes, it is to be a pattern for each individual who chases after Jesus, and it is sure to rekindle a dormant faith if that is what is needed. Moreover, the church, collectively, must model countercultural humility. In an age of celebrity Christianity, the cross calls us to lay down platforms and pick up basins and towels.

Paul warned the Galatians not to "use your freedom to indulge the flesh" but to "serve one another humbly in love" (Gal. 5:13 NIV). A church marked by humility is a community where joy multiplies. Let us labor not for influence, but for fruit. Not for visibility, but for faithfulness. That is the soil where revival grows. Want to change your church? Serve in the humility of Christ. Promote a culture of freewheeling humble service to others and the community. Remember that first snapshot of the early church in Acts 2? Whatever they had—they let it go for the sake of others. "They sold property and possessions to give to anyone who had need" (Acts 2:45 NIV). A spirit of humble service and generosity go hand in hand.

THE JOY SET BEFORE US

Hebrews 12:2 reminds us of Jesus: "For the joy set before him he endured the cross" (NIV). Joy and humility are not mutually exclusive—they are married in the gospel. Again, Jesus led the way and showed us the connection between humble obedience and joy. The joy set before Him was the prospect of seeing countless future generations of humble believers living out their faith with joyful obedience. The joy set before Him was costly. To walk in humility is to follow Jesus to the cross of a sacrificial life. Joy does not lie in recognition, but in obedience.

I'll close with a story I've always loved to tell. I don't care how many times I have heard it or told it, it reminds me of who we are, and who He is:

> *The captain of the ship looked into the dark night and saw faint lights in the distance. Immediately, he told his signalman to send a message: "Alter your course 10 degrees south."*
>
> *Promptly, a return message was received: "Alter your course 10 degrees north."*
>
> *The captain was angered; his command had been ignored. So he sent a second message: "Alter your course 10 degrees south—I am the captain!"*
>
> *Soon another message was received: "Alter your course 10 degrees north—I am seaman third class Jones."*
>
> *Immediately, the captain sent a third message, knowing the fear it would evoke: "Alter your course 10 degrees south—I am a battleship!"*
>
> *Then the reply came: "Alter your course 10 degrees north—I am a lighthouse."*[2]

I'm involved with a seminary that trains pastors and ministry leaders and sadly, over the years, I've seen more than a few students learn—often the hard way—the consequences of disregarding God's commands. Some have faced ruined marriages, faltering ministries, and even shipwrecked faith. Thankfully, these cases are rare, but even one is too many. The good news is that there is always a safe harbor of grace and forgiveness. Anyone with a repentant heart and a willingness to chart a new course can return to a humble, joyful, and rekindled faith.

Are your embers dim? Are you desiring to have a faith on fire? If so, I urge you prayerfully to consider rekindling the joy of your faith by pursuing a humble and genuine selflessness before God and those you serve. Trust me: you will never regret the change of course. Jesus Christ is the lighthouse. He knows best. He has modeled it for us. He will never steer you wrong.

A PRAYER FOR HUMBLE JOY

I've not done this a lot, but I feel the need to commit this one to the Lord in prayer.

> *Lord Jesus, You are the humble King, who stooped to save, who knelt to serve, who died to give life. Teach me to follow Your way. Rid me of pride, of the need to be seen, and of the hunger for applause. Make me one who rejoices in serving, who lowers myself to lift others. Let the joy of Your humility be mine. Rekindle my heart with the fire of quiet obedience and hidden faithfulness. In Your name, the Name above every name, I pray. Amen.*

REKINDLED THROUGH THE CROSS

The pathway to renewed joy is not paved with promotion, but with surrender. The fire of faith is fanned in the humble heart, the one that bends low to lift high the name of Jesus. Let us listen and respond humbly to the words of Micah: "What does the Lord require of you? To act justly and to love mercy and to walk humbly with your God" (Micah 6:8 NIV).

Walk humbly. Serve joyfully. Rekindle your heart through the beautiful descent of Christlike humility.

MORE KINDLING . . .

Take a few moments to prayerfully ask yourself some open-ended questions . . .

1. Where is pride quietly operating in my life? Who might I invite into my life to help me answer that question?
2. When was the last time I served with no recognition or reward simply out of humble worship for the Lord? How did that make me feel about my faith?
3. What would it look like to pursue humility practically at home or in my place of ministry?
4. How might a life of sacrificial service restore my joy in Christ?

6

REKINDLED ZEAL

A Burden for the World

"For this is how God loved the world: He gave his one and only Son, so that everyone who believes in him will not perish but have eternal life."

JOHN 3:16

The final essential to revive your faith is close to my heart. As a seminary president, I have the privilege of traveling the world to speak and teach in many environments such as churches, conferences, conventions. It's always a joy to visit alumni serving in some of the most challenging places on the planet. Inevitably, after a long season of teaching, speaking and, at times, carrying out painfully monotonous administrative tasks, my passion for spiritual things can begin to fade. If I'm not careful, I can find myself tempted to disengage from the things of the Lord and waste time on distractions that have little lasting value.

However, as soon as I step off the plane and enter the lives and cultures of people from other parts of the world, my heart revives. It's not magic, it is spiritual. I feel renewed energy and motivation because it always seems like I'm right in the center of God's passion and heartbeat. As I write this chapter, I am on the heels of a significant global gathering of believers, and I am exhausted yet energized. Hearing the stories of the movements of God throughout the world is overwhelming. He is at work. He is alive, and we dare not forget it. I've been in places recently where many people are coming to faith. I've seen it. It's real.

Few things fan the flame of faith like sharing Christ with the world. It rekindles my fire every single time. That makes sense because the God we serve sent His only Son to die for a lost and rebellious world. Our God has a passion for the world (John 3:16). So must we.

THE REKINDLED JOY FROM A MISSION-DRIVEN LIFE

There is no greater joy in the Christian life than joining God in His redemptive mission. Sharing the message of Christ with the world is not a burdensome duty—it is the overflow of a heart captivated by God's grace. The sixth essential to rekindling our faith is deepening a passion for proclaiming Jesus to all people, near and far. When our hearts beat in rhythm with God's global purposes, our faith is energized, our joy renewed, and our lives grow more closely aligned with His eternal purposes in Christ.

Psalm 67 gives us a glimpse of the missionary heartbeat of God in the Old Testament, revealing how God's blessings were never meant to terminate with Israel, but rather to flow through them to all nations. The nation of Israel was always called and positioned to be a "kingdom of priests" (Ex. 19:6). They were to be representatives to the world of how to live, serve, and depend on the Creator of the universe. Psalm 67 is a prayer for the spread of God's fame so that His saving power would be known "among people everywhere" (v. 2).

Read aloud the words of the psalmist, which capture the passion of God for the world He made:

> *May God be merciful and bless us. May his face smile with favor on us. May your ways be known throughout the earth, your saving power among people everywhere. May the nations praise you, O God. Yes, may all the nations praise you. Let the whole world sing for joy because you govern the nations with justice and guide the people of the whole world. May the nations praise you, O God. Yes, may all the nations praise you. Then the earth will yield its harvests, and God, our God, will richly bless us. Yes, God will bless us, and people all over the world will fear him.*

It's hard to read that psalm and walk away unconvinced of God's passion for the world—for the *people* of the whole world. All the nations on the planet are in God's loving and gracious gaze. His heart burns for the world and the people He created. He longs for everyone everywhere to receive the grace and freedom of Jesus and the joyous grace that flows from His Name!

I was running on fumes. It was at that moment when the flame of passion was starting to fade.

When we realign our hearts with the heartbeat of God, the joy of our salvation begins to return. Our faith is reignited in powerful, often unexpected ways as we connect with what God is doing in the world—especially as we align ourselves with His deep love for the nations. In 2024, several colleagues and I flew to Liberia. Our mission was to encourage a handful of recent seminary graduates in that part of Africa. Specifically, we spent time with the entire team at the Evangelical Seminary of West Africa. While there, we also led a conference for Liberian pastors to help them understand and apply the Bible as one grand story. We call it *The Story of Scripture*. It was a wonderfully busy season. That trip coincided with the beginning of a yearlong celebration of Dallas Theological Seminary's centennial. We had spent the previous year or more planning and putting multiple layers of communications, messages, and events in place.

The year had been filled with meetings, along with my regular teaching and administrative responsibilities. Coupled with all of that, I had suffered a sudden torn disk in my back months before that put me out of commission for six weeks! Needless to say, I was running on fumes. It was at that moment when the flame of passion was starting to fade. It can happen to any of us during times of exhaustion. Well, that's where I was—on the west coast of Africa.

It was there I stepped in front of six hundred biblically hungry Liberian pastors and ministry leaders eager to participate in *The Story of Scripture* experience. As they began to worship and dance (literally) and offer joyful praise to God, the embers of my faith began to burn more brightly. I found myself lost in the moment. My heart soared. It was Liberia, remember, which meant it was hot. Did I mention hot? We clocked it, friends—it was 120 degrees (Fahrenheit) on stage at one point! However, it might as well have been a cool 60 degrees because I felt so spiritually alive, and in tune with the very heart of God. The power of serving the nations had started to fan my smoldering spirit.

This sixth essential reminds us of God's passion for people everywhere. The entirety of Holy Scripture, from Genesis to Revelation, challenges us to revive a deep desire for sharing

Christ with the nations—both near and far, around the world, and even from your backyard fence. We are now going to see 1) how this passion flows from God's character, 2) how Jesus modeled it in His earthly ministry, and 3) how the church today is called to embrace its global commission.

GOD'S HEART FOR THE NATIONS IN THE OLD TESTAMENT

Many believers think of evangelism and missions as primarily a New Testament concept. After all, Jesus did say, "Go and make disciples of all the nations" (Matt. 28:19). Undoubtedly, we will get to that critical statement. However, the truth is, God's heart for the nations has been present from the beginning.

The Promise to Abraham: Blessing for All People (Genesis 12:1–3)

As we have already seen, when God called Abraham, He presented an almost melodic promise stating that through Abram would come a people (the Jewish nation) residing in a designated place (the land of Israel) who would bless the world. The final promise encompassed His love for all nations: "All peoples on earth will be blessed through you" (v. 3 NIV). God intended from the beginning that His covenant people would be a conduit through whom His lavish, unending grace would flow to all nations.

In my travels, I see the evidence of His grace pouring out on ministries, churches, and schools committed to serving and exalting Jesus Christ as Lord. I see it in His provision for pastors and missionaries laboring faithfully and sacrificially in other countries and among ethnic communities in the cities of America also.

The imprint of grace given to Abraham thousands of years ago remains evident in the hearts and passions of believers from every tribe and nation. That must light your fire! This promise is repeated throughout Genesis (22:18; 26:4; 28:14), revealing God's consistent desire for all the families of the earth to know Him.

And it continues to the prophets . . .

Israel as a Light to the Nations (Isaiah 49:6)

God declared to the prophet Isaiah, "You will do more than restore the people of Israel to me. I will make you a light to the Gentiles, and you will bring my salvation to the ends of the earth." Did you notice the connection between Israel's heart being rekindled for the Lord and the reach of grace across to the hearts of Gentiles? Seeing God's loving and gracious heart and its power to "restore" Israel's passion for the Lord is a joy!

By the time the Lord spoke to Isaiah, Israel had languished in a dry and barren wilderness of sin, and the nation's collective flame of faith had grown shockingly dim. God determined to use the bold and pointed preaching of Isaiah to reignite that flame of faith and to allow it to spread like a fire to the Gentiles. His prophetic word made it clear that Israel's calling was never about keeping His blessings to themselves. They were to shine His light outward, revealing His glory to the nations. Chosen by grace, they were called to reflect that grace to others.

I have spent much time in the land of Israel. Come and travel there with me. I may say this with a smile, but I mean it: It is God's will for you to go to Israel! Plan on it. Save your shekels, friends. It will make the Bible come alive. When you go, you might be struck by the barren, arid geography and climate. Ultimately, there is nothing barren about that land. You'll soon discover the vibrant evidence of the gospel's light—Greek Christians worshiping on the Mount of Olives, and Japanese, Korean, Indian, and Russian believers baptizing new converts in the sparkling waters of the Jordan River. In Bethlehem, the ancient city of the Messiah's birth, followers of Jesus gather to reflect on the meaning of their faith. Even in a nation that for now has rejected her Messiah, the light of Jesus Christ sparks a rekindled heart for God to all people everywhere.

Most travelers are moved by being in the hallowed places where Jesus once walked and served the neediest of that time. It is historical for sure. Facts are plenty when I lead new pilgrims to Israel because I want them to receive the "goods" of thorough Bible teaching and the basics of Bible geography.

However, time after time, some Christians who join me come with a dryness to their faith, only to experience a rekindled joy as they witness believers from around the world worshiping our risen Savior. This is evidence of the power of the gospel for the nations. They return to their homes and churches renewed with a revived faith and boldness for reaching the world for Christ. Israel is ground zero of God's plans for witnessing to all the nations.

God's Glory Among the Nations in the Psalms

This passion for the nations also emerges in the worship songs of God's people, embedded in the Old Testament book of Psalms. In many ways, the book of Psalms is the hymnbook of faith for the people of God. And these beautifully crafted songs give us a glimpse into God's heart. Read three select passages:

> *The poor will eat and be satisfied. All who seek the LORD will praise him. Their hearts will rejoice with everlasting joy. The whole earth will acknowledge the LORD and return to him. All the families of the nations will bow down before him.* (PS. 22:26–27)

> *All the nations you made will come and bow before you, LORD; they will praise your holy name. For you are great and perform wonderful deeds. You alone are God.* (PS. 86:9–10)

> *Sing a new song to the* Lord*! Let the whole earth sing to the* Lord*! Sing to the* Lord*; praise his name. Each day proclaim the good news that he saves. Publish his glorious deeds among the nations. Tell everyone about the amazing things he does.* (Ps. 96:1–3)

Do you see the connection between returning to the Lord, bringing His name to the nations, and experiencing a rekindled joy? The worship songs of God's people make it clear that God's blessing is not a private privilege but a platform for proclamation and an opportunity to live out a heart of joy for the world He made. That is always true of God's grace. His love and kindness have been poured out on us, not just for our benefit but for the benefit of others. It is for the benefit of all the listening and observing audience. We never should live it out just to impress others; but rather to encourage onlookers to "taste and see that the Lord is good!" (Ps. 34:8 esv).

GOD'S HEART FOR THE NATIONS: HOW JONAH TELLS THE TALE

The book of Jonah is often remembered for its dramatic storyline and the great fish that swallows the reluctant prophet. However, it offers far more than an exciting tale. Trust me—it is much more than a tale of a whale. It's an account of a genuine prophet who was given an absolute command to take God's word into the heart of the Assyrian empire. Why? Because God cares for the nations. Judgment is real, and God longs for all to turn to Him—even the Assyrians. Beneath the book of Jonah's narrative is a profound theological message about the character of God—His relentless compassion, His pursuit of the lost, and His heart for all peoples, not just Israel.

When the story opens, Jonah is not in a good place. A believer for sure, he had grown detached from the things of the Lord. That can be understood from his initial response to God's command to leave his comfort zone and travel to a distant land with a message from the Lord.

As we explore the book of Jonah, we see a striking foreshadowing of Jesus Christ, who, unlike Jonah, willingly left His home in heaven to save sinners. The call for Christians to live out this mission mirrors the heart of God displayed both in Jonah and in Jesus. That call is to rekindle in us the joy and purpose of our faith.

The Call of Jonah

Jonah begins with a divine commission: "Go to the great city of Nineveh and preach against it, because its wickedness has come up before me" (Jonah 1:2 NIV). Nineveh was the capital of Assyria, Israel's enemy, known for its brutality and idolatry. The call to preach to Nineveh would have struck Jonah as undesirable and *outrageous*. Why would God offer mercy to the enemies of His people?

Jonah's response was flight, not faith. How incredibly honest is the Lord in His Word! It shows the frailty of human faith that, at times, grows unresponsive to His gracious ways. Often it demonstrates a bold rejection of God's compassion for people. "But Jonah ran away from the LORD and headed for Tarshish" (1:3 NIV). Rather than move toward the need and the calling of God, Jonah moved in the opposite direction, geographically and spiritually. His disobedience exposes a deeper heart issue—a narrow understanding of God's mercy and resistance to His universal compassion.

That's what happens when our faith grows dry and barren. We lose our zeal for the things of the Lord. We flatline in our responses to Him and we are dulled to His voice. Call it what it is: We can find ourselves in seasons without God's perspective and passion. We fail to look up and see the world and the people of the world as God sees them: individuals He is pursuing.

SPIRITUAL TWALKING

Have you heard of "twalking"? This coined word describes being distracted by posting, talking, or texting on a cellphone while walking, sometimes with unfortunate consequences. So-called phone zombies have bumped into one other, and many pedestrians have been injured or worse when their heads are looking down and they're unaware of their surroundings.

While the pitfalls and problems of cellphone twalking are real, "spiritual twalking" presents an equally clear and present danger. Unfortunately, many believers today live with their heads down instead of up because we get weighed down by the stuff of this world. When we do, we forget to focus on what matters most to God.

Social agendas sensationalize and drive much of the news, social media, and political propaganda we consume. These media outlets compete for our allegiance and continually encourage us to gaze at things below rather than things above. I think now we are paying the price. True, we are responsible for engaging in public discourse, both as people who make and are made by culture; but as believers we are specifically called to be salt and light. When we fixate our attention on every dispute and feel obliged to provide our limited opinions on the latest crisis in this fallen world, we forget what the Bible says and the *hope* that it offers. When Christ followers fail to look up, we frequently fall; this results from spiritual twalking.

REMEMBER TO LOOK UP

The Bible calls believers in the Lord Jesus to look *up* for clarity while living below. Listen to what Paul says in Colossians 3:1–2 (NIV): "Since, then, you have been raised with Christ, set your hearts on things above, where Christ is, seated at the right hand of God. Set your minds on things above, not on earthly things."

Under the direction of the Holy Spirit, Paul's charge is clear and pointed. He encourages us to *remember* something extremely valuable and then challenges us to *act* on that remembrance. First, the apostle encourages believers to *remember* that we "have been raised with Christ." He continues the discussion in Colossians 2:12–13 (NIV) when he recalls that we were "buried" with Christ and thus dead to sin. Being buried means death *to the world's belief system* (Col. 2:20). With that reality in mind, he then stresses the totality of the gospel: death, burial, *and* resurrection.

Our being raised with Christ is certain, grounded in the unwavering promise of His victory over death. The picture is strong. God sits on his throne, and the exalted Christ sits at His right hand in a position of power, prominence, and protection. James Dunn states, "The consequences for the Christian perspective are thus also clear. If Jesus, the Christ, is so highly favored and acknowledged to be God's 'right-hand man,' with all the power and authority to effect God's will and to protect his own which is implicit in that claim, then Christian life should be entirely oriented by reference to this Christ."[1]

Second, the reality of being raised with Christ challenges us to *act* on that remembrance and to do so regularly. Did you note that Paul twice calls us to look up in this brief passage? In Colossians 3:1, the charge is to "set your *hearts* on things above" (NIV; emphasis added). In referencing our "hearts," Paul speaks to our desires, which are now bent toward heaven in light of being unified with the risen Savior. God transforms us through our union with Him. This relationship changes our moral viewpoint, which should be from a position of redemption, and not driven by earthly patterns.

In Colossians 3:2 (NIV), he repeats the charge with a twist. We are to set our "minds" on things above. This second statement addresses our thoughts. It implies assessing the time and passion we dedicate to our thinking and the actions that follow from those thoughts. To avoid confusion, Paul states we are to engage our minds on "things above," not on "earthly things," that is, things of the world. The contrast to the first admonition is that our focus should be on what is up (heaven), not down (earth).

Here, as much as anywhere, the twofold perspective of believers appears. We live in two domains: the fallen order and the redeemed order, a division Paul had already explained in Colossians 1:15–20. While existing in this broken world, we are not to let it occupy our perspective. Our values should point heavenward.

Invasive Action to Avoid Spiritual Twalking

Do you need a dose of encouragement today? Take heart, my friends. God's got this. Jesus has been exalted, and we are unified with Him by grace through faith. Our priorities in engaging one another in the world are fundamentally shaped by the fact that God has raised us up with Christ and that He (Christ) is now seated at the Father's right hand.

When the world around us falls apart and human systems come crashing down, remember that we stand with the resurrected Savior! As Bible scholar William Barclay aptly stated, "From now on, the Christian will see everything in the light and against the background of eternity. He will no longer live as if this world mattered; he will see this world against the background of the larger world of eternity."[2]

That reality makes a difference today. It reminds us that God is concerned about people, not things. It forces us to focus on what matters—even amid the storms of life. When facing the world's problems, including plagues, pestilence, violence, injustice, social wrongs, and faulty political systems, we know the risen Lord is the Lord over all. He has a plan that He is working to His ends. Ultimately, all wrongs will be made right; sin will be no more, and God's rule, through his appointed Christ, will be manifest in heaven *and* on the re-created earth. Despite what our eyes see, faith leads us to trust in Him even when the present circumstances and pundits say it is foolish.

What's true for us all is the constant need to purge ourselves of the input of the world and refill our hearts and minds with the things of God.

Does that mean we should not be active in addressing the world's problems? By no means. It means our thoughts and actions should be heaven-centric as we do it. This means we should focus on taking as many people as possible to heaven. We are called to *live* this gospel as we share it with others. When we do, it *will* invigorate us in untold ways. It will fire up our faith in ways that nothing else can.

Paul also charges us to *act* in that same passage by looking up. We begin by assessing where we fixate our hearts and minds, and then respond accordingly. For some, looking up requires significant adjustments to interacting in the public square. For others, looking up means we need to spend more time studying and applying the Word to our lives than conforming to the narrative of the world. For others still, looking up means living out the gospel of Jesus Christ in word and deed instead of defaulting to earthly patterns of discourse that, although promising good, will ultimately fail. What's true for us all is the constant need to purge ourselves of the input of the world and refill our hearts and minds with the things of God. We need His passion and perspective. That is why Paul admonishes believers not to conform to the world but instead renew our minds, changing the way we think to conform to God's perspective (Rom. 12:1–2).

The benefits of doing so are immense. When we do, we will remember that God is sovereign, our salvation is secure, the best is yet to come, and we need to share that with other people and nations. Come on, Christ followers, we can do this. Let's stop spiritual twalking. Let's keep our focus on the things above. It makes all the difference in (and for) the world.

As all of this relates to Jonah, he didn't keep his head up. As the story goes—he goes down. But even in a downward spiral . . . God pursued him just like He does with you and me.

God's Sovereignty and Mercy in Pursuit

As Jonah flees, God pursues. He sends a storm (Jonah 1:4), prepares a great fish (1:17), and sustains Jonah in the belly of that fish for three days. That's a ton of activity from God to rescue Jonah from his unresponsive heart! God cares deeply about our smoldering faith. He has so much invested in our salvation because of the enormous sacrifice of his Son, Jesus, that He won't allow us to linger in a constant and deepening spiritual decline. He pursues not mercilessly but mercifully! That's what happens to Jonah. He cannot escape the mercy of God even though God shows it initially by literally *hurling* a storm the prophet's way.

Once Jonah goes overboard in his rebellion, God is not done. In the fish, Jonah prays a heartfelt prayer, ending with the powerful declaration: "My salvation comes from the LORD" (2:9). Ironically, Jonah confesses this while still not fully understanding the scope of God's saving intent. And he states it while never fully confessing his rebellious heart.

When Jonah is given a second chance and obeys the call (3:1–3), he delivers a barebones message: "Forty days from now Nineveh will be destroyed!" (3:4). There is no mention of grace or repentance. Yet remarkably, the people of Nineveh respond; they fast, repent, and cry out for mercy (3:5–9). "When God saw what they did . . . he relented and did not bring on them the destruction he had threatened" (3:10 NIV).

This is perhaps the most stunning moment of the book: God relents. His heart is moved by repentance, which reveals a clear window into the heart of God. He is slow to anger, abounding in love, and willing to forgive all who turn to Him.

This makes me think of another joyful declaration from God through the pen of the apostle Paul, no stranger to the impact of grace. While steeped in rebellion, the living Jesus appeared to him and commissioned him to take this message of mercy to the Gentile world:

> *God made Christ, who never sinned, to be the offering for our sin, so that we could be made right with God through Christ.* (2 COR. 5:21)

The flame of the gospel for the Gentiles had been lit in the heart of Paul. And the world was never the same. That was supposed to have happened to Jonah. And it is supposed to happen to us too.

Jonah's Anger and God's Compassion

Chapter 4 shifts focus from Nineveh to Jonah's heart. Jonah is furious, his heart still dry. His faith smoldering in cynicism:

"Didn't I say before I left home that you would do this, Lord? *That is why I ran away to Tarshish! I knew that you are a merciful and compassionate God, slow to get angry and filled with unfailing love."* (v. 2)

Jonah resents God's compassion. He would rather die than see his enemies forgiven. His barren faith clashed with the vibrant heart of God for the people of Nineveh. God then appoints a plant to provide Jonah shade and, just as quickly, appoints a worm to destroy it. When Jonah complains about the loss of the plant, God delivers the final lesson:

"Should I not have concern for the great city of Nineveh, in which there are more than a hundred and twenty thousand people who cannot tell their right hand from their left—and also many animals?" (v.11 NIV)

Jonah's story ends with a question left in the air: Will Jonah and the reader embrace God's heart for the nations? Will you? Will I?

JONAH AND JESUS: A GREATER MISSIONARY

Jesus Himself draws a connection between Jonah and His ministry. In Matthew 12:40 (NIV), He says, "For as Jonah was three days and three nights in the belly of a huge fish, so the Son of Man will be three days and three nights in the heart of the earth."

But while Jonah fled from God's call, Jesus embraced it fully. And that embrace lit a flame of joy that can be ours too.

We do this by keeping our eyes on Jesus [Remember—we have to look up!], the champion who initiates and perfects our faith. Because of the joy awaiting him, he endured the cross, disregarding its shame. Now he is seated in the place of honor beside God's throne. (HEB. 12:2)

There is a clear connection between the joy we experience in our faith when we are related to Jesus and His heart for the world. He endured so much in His journey to provide salvation, but it was the joy of knowing that one day people from every tribe and tongue would have the opportunity to be reconciled with God that spurred Jesus to finish the work of the cross.

It must be proclaimed clearly that Jesus leaving heaven to dwell among sinners is the ultimate missionary journey. While Jonah fled from a city of enemies, Jesus ran toward a world that ultimately rejected Him. He bore the full weight of sin not just for Israel but for every nation, tribe, and tongue. Jesus' life, death, and resurrection are the ultimate demonstrations of God's compassion and become the source of rekindled joy for all of us whose faith has grown dry.

In Jonah, we see a reluctant prophet who needed to be thrown into the sea to calm a storm of judgment. In Jesus, we see a willing Savior who calmed the storm of sin's condemnation by offering Himself as a sacrifice. A fish swallowed Jonah; Jesus was swallowed by death itself— and both emerged after three days, but only Jesus emerged victorious, never to die again.

Jonah's message led to repentance in Nineveh, but Jesus' message and resurrection power bring salvation to all who believe and embrace it. He is the better Jonah. He did not flee from sinners; instead, He ensured eternal fellowship with them.

GOD'S HEART, OUR MISSION

If God's compassion extends beyond man-made borders, then so must ours. Christians are called to be missionaries—not all in the formal sense of overseas ministry, but in the sense that we are sent people. And when we engage with God and enter His heart for the world, our faith is revived. We can experience that same joy Jesus did as He went to the cross. The goal is worth the cost!

Jesus said, "As the Father has sent me, so I am sending you" (John 20:21). We are sent to go into the world, just as Jesus was sent from heaven and just as Jonah was sent to Nineveh.

The gospel calls us to love our enemies, serve those who don't deserve it, go where it's uncomfortable, and reflect God's boundless mercy. It is easy to fall into Jonah's desert of an unresponsive heart, content to receive grace for ourselves but slow to extend it to others, especially those who are different, antagonistic, or complex. The heart of God beats for all people, for the world.

This missional calling is not a burden but a joy. Going into the world with the gospel refreshes our joy and happiness. It enlivens our hearts with the things that God cares about deeply. When we align our hearts with God's heart for the world, we rediscover the joy of our faith. Evangelism and mission are not just duties; they are invitations to participate in the most extraordinary story of redemption the world has ever known.

REKINDLING THE JOY OF OUR FAITH

Many believers experience seasons of dryness, when faith feels routine or heavy. Often, this is linked to a disconnect from God's mission. Jonah, when inwardly focused and resistant to God's plan, was miserable—even suicidal. However, when we step into the stream of God's compassion, we find ourselves renewed.

Just as Jesus told His disciples, "My food . . . is to do the will of him who sent me" (John 4:34 NIV), so too will we be nourished when we serve God's heart for the nations. Evangelism is not just about others receiving Good News; it's about us living in it. When we see God change lives—sinners repent, hearts heal, communities transform—we taste the joy of heaven. The Bible says, "There is rejoicing in the presence of the angels of God over one sinner who repents" (Luke 15:10 NIV).

Jonah ends with an unresolved question because it is meant to leave us pondering: Will we stay under the withered plant of self-centered religion, or will we rise and go with God to the city with a rekindled heart of compassion and joy for people?

THE MISSION OF CHRIST: FROM INCARNATION TO COMMISSION

When Jesus stepped into human history, He did so with a clear mission: "The Son of Man came to seek and save those who are lost" (Luke 19:10). His ministry was clearly among the nations. Though centered in Israel, Jesus constantly foreshadowed the global scope of His kingdom:

> *He praised the faith of a Roman centurion.* (MATT. 8:8–10)
>
> *He ministered to a Samaritan woman, bringing an entire village to faith.* (JOHN 4)
>
> *He healed a Canaanite woman's daughter.* (MATT. 15:28)

These moments revealed that the grace of God was not confined by ethnicity or geography. It was for the whole world. Remember? "For God so loved *the world*" (John 3:16 NIV; emphasis added). And upon Jesus' departure, He made it clear that salvation is for all. It's for the nations. For all people.

The Great Commission (Matthew 28:18–20)

After His resurrection, Jesus gave His followers their marching orders: "All authority in heaven and on earth has been given to me. Therefore go and make disciples of all nations, baptizing them in the name of the Father and of the Son and the Holy Spirit, and teaching them to obey everything I have commanded you. And surely I am with you always, to the very end of the age."

The command was clear, comprehensive, and cosmic in scope.

The Greek word for "nations" refers to all ethnic groups. Jesus' final words to His disciples were not suggestions but a commission (make disciples of all nations) rooted in His authority and framed by His presence "I am with you always, to the very end of the age."

The Fields Are Ready for Harvest (John 4:35)

After His interaction with the Samaritan woman, Jesus told His disciples: "Open your eyes and look at the fields! They are ripe for harvest" (NIV). In other words, the mission is urgent, and the time is now. Here is what we need to remember: The heart of Jesus beats for the lost. His joy was to do the Father's will. The bottom line is that, as His followers, our joy is rekindled when we share His mission. It is purposeful (all sinners need the Savior) and powerful (all those saved are strengthened when they share the Good News).

THE EARLY CHURCH AND THE SPREAD OF THE GOSPEL

The book of Acts is the story of a Spirit-empowered church spreading the message of Christ from Jerusalem to the ends of the earth. It's worth reminding ourselves how they, the early church, focused on what mattered most. We get snapshots of how they zeroed in on the heart of God.

Pentecost and the Multilingual Church (Acts 2)

The first great missionary moment after the resurrection came at Pentecost when people from every nation under heaven heard the gospel in their own language. This was no accident. God was declaring that the gospel is for all people. It was undoubtedly an act of God. He performed a miracle for sure; but He also was delivering a message. The gospel is for all who will believe.

Antioch: A Sending Church (Acts 13) and Missionary Journeys

The Antioch church, comprising diverse leaders and members, became the launching pad for global missions. They fasted, prayed, and sent Paul and Barnabas. This local church understood its global responsibility—and every church should. We see this same conviction in the life of the apostle Paul, whose passion burned for those who had never heard the name of Jesus. Consider his words to the church in Rome: "It has always been my ambition to preach the gospel where Christ was not known" (Rom. 15:20 NIV). That singular aim—to make Christ known among the nations—was the driving force behind all of his missionary journeys.

THE FINAL VISION: EVERY NATION BEFORE THE THRONE

The last book of the Bible gives us a breathtaking picture of the mission *fulfilled* and the inexhaustible flame of joy it sparks even into eternity:

> *After this I looked, and there before me was a great multitude that no one could count, from every nation, tribe, people and language, standing before the throne and before the Lamb.* (REV. 7:9 NIV)

What a picture! This is the endgame of history—a multiethnic choir praising the Redeemer. Missions are not a manufactured project; it is God's eternal plan. And it will not fail. Satan does not win!

HOW A REKINDLED HEART FOR THE WORLD REKINDLES JOY

Evangelism—sharing our faith in Christ—is not merely a responsibility; it is a wellspring of *joy*. And it's not just for those in vocational Christian ministry. All believers are in ministry! All are called to share and live out the Good News. We should care about proclaiming God's grace. Friends, it is excellent news. Note how the Bible connects "joy" with salvation. Three quick passages come to mind.

There's Joy in Heaven!

You'll remember what Jesus said: "There is rejoicing in the presence of the angels of God over one sinner who repents" (Luke 15:10 NIV). If heaven throws a party for sinners who have been found, should we not as well?

There's Joy in the Impact of the Gospel

The gospel itself is the power of God for salvation. When we share it, we are unleashing life-transforming truth. Hearts are changed. Lives are made new. And watching someone come alive in Christ is pure, unfiltered joy. Remember the beggar that Peter and John encountered on their way to the temple? After being healed, his response was unforgettable: "He jumped up, stood on his feet, and began to walk! Then, walking, leaping, and praising God, he went into the Temple with them" (Acts 3:8). Imagine witnessing that moment—the sheer joy, the awe, the transformation. That kind of response still happens. All over the world. Every single day. This is the power of the gospel at work—everywhere. Christians! God has given us a piece of the action!

There's Joy in Obedience

Jesus said, "If you keep my commands, you will remain in my love. . . . I have told you this so that my joy may be in you" (John 15:10–11 NIV). While these words apply to all His commands, they are especially true when it comes to sharing and living out the gospel. In other words, this promise—the joy of Christ dwelling in us—is given to those who zealously pursue God's heart for the nations. A passion for the lost will reignite the fire of your faith. Why? Because it shifts your focus back to the joy of your own salvation—a joy worth sharing.

REKINDLING PASSION FOR EVANGELISM IN THE CHURCH

Missions begin when we call upon the Lord for the nations. Here are some compelling, somber reminders from God's Word.

> *Satan, who is the god of this world, has blinded the minds of those who don't believe. They are unable to see the glorious light of the Good News. They don't understand this message about the glory of Christ, who is the exact likeness of God.* (2 COR. 4:4)

A sure way to rekindle your heart for people is to pray that God would heal their spiritual blindness so they can see the light of Christ's glory when they hear the gospel. As you pray, your heart softens, and you begin to experience renewed joy knowing that God is faithful to answer prayer.

We also can pray for those in dark and perilous places, asking that the Lord grant them courage to speak the name of Christ boldly, no matter the cost. Paul wrote,

> *And pray for me, too. Ask God to give me the right words so I can boldly explain God's mysterious plan that the Good News is for Jews and Gentiles alike. I am in chains now, still preaching this message as God's ambassador. So pray that I will keep on speaking boldly for him, as I should.* (EPH. 6:19–20)

Pray for courage for our brothers and sisters in Christ worldwide who share the Good News. Pray that their efforts begin a work in you to rekindle you and ignite your joy in being a part of God's plan to reach the nations.

As this chapter concludes, it is helpful to return to where we started. Psalm 67 concludes with a triumphant vision: "Let the whole world sing for joy, because you govern the nations with justice and guide the people of the whole world" (v. 4). The joy of the Lord is our strength. That is undoubtedly true. However, that joy expands when we align our hearts with God's global mission. Let us be people who rejoice not just in our salvation but also in the salvation of all of the world. When you do, the fire of your faith will be rekindled. It will begin to burn brightly. Let the nations be glad. Let the church be bold. Let the lost be found. And let joy abound in every heart set aflame by the gospel of Christ . . . everywhere!

MORE KINDLING . . .

1. Who are three people you can pray for and intentionally engage with the gospel?

2. How can you leverage your time, professional skills, vocation, and resources for world missions?

3. Where might God call you to go—short-term, mid-term, or long-term? Get your passport and go!

4. How can you be a catalyst for joyful compassion for the world in your local church?

5. What steps can you take to reignite your passion for the world?

THE END . . .

But Only the Beginning

Somehow, the Lord brought you to this book and now you are reading the final few paragraphs. Whether you read it all in one lump sum or piecemeal it together, here you are—The End.

Along the way, I pray you have heard my argument. You've also listened to my musings! Every writer seems to string together some of their life's *experiences* and attempts to connect to life's *realities.* As a Christ follower, those experiences and understanding of reality must be directed and informed by God's Word. That's where I am regarding the rekindling of our faith.

This topic is near to me because, as a Christian, I've had a weak fire of faith in the past. Who hasn't? It is a reality in this fallen world—even for the redeemed, those saved by grace through faith in Christ. The fire dims, and the flames subside. We don't always find ourselves on the mountain tops, clicking on all cylinders and running at max capacity of our spiritual existence. The exuberance of initial conversion faith can wane.

Even mature believers can find themselves in bad ruts. It will happen because life happens.

If your current walk with the Lord has diminished, don't beat yourself up. You receive no condemnation from me. I hope it is just the opposite. I pray that you have received encouragement from this book. Oh, for sure, the Spirit may convict. I pray He has. It's possible that while reading these pages, you sensed a prodding from God to stoke the fire and fan the flame, and a few helpful essentials for doing that. Maybe you felt led to dig up those embers right below the surface so that they can be used for their intended purpose—to ignite a vibrant fire. If you have sensed the tug of God as we have made this journey together, may I encourage you not to run from His leading? May I be so bold as to say it more aggressively? Don't ignore His promptings.

If your current walk with the Lord has diminished, don't beat yourself up. I pray that you have received encouragement from this book.

In Christian circles, we often hear the phrase, "Don't quench the Spirit." It's very appropriate in a discussion like ours—a conversation where we are talking about "fire" as a metaphor for the vibrancy of our faith. "Stifle the Spirit" is a phrase that comes from 1 Thessalonians 5:16–19. Listen to what Paul says in that context to the church at Thessalonica:

> *Always be joyful. Never stop praying. Be thankful in all circumstances, for this is God's will for you who belong to Christ Jesus. Do not stifle the Holy Spirit.*

What a powerful passage! Think of what Paul is saying to his friends at the church in Thessalonica. This church had challenges.

They had been walking faithfully but were now living in the face of persecution. Paul wrote to encourage them to continue growing in their godliness and avoid errant teachings from those opposing Christ. In this set of letters (1 and 2 Thessalonians), Paul reminded them to live every day in light of the return of the Lord. That is motivation!

But just think about what he says in the verses quoted above, which come at the end of His first letter. Be joyful (v. 16). Be prayerful (v. 17).

Be thankful (v. 18). And *don't* stifle the Spirit (v. 19). The word as used in our translation above, "stifle," is in other translations as "quench." This verb is used elsewhere in the Bible to imply extinguishing a fire. That's the background of the word. Indeed, in the context of 1 Thessalonians 5, Paul was challenging the church to adhere to words of edification, exhortation, and encouragement. He told them, "Don't suppress the work of the Spirit in church." That is also true for you and me personally.

We dare not "quench" (stifle, suppress, extinguish) the prodding of the Holy Spirit. If God has challenged you to fan your flame of salvation—do it! Get the most enormous fan you can find. Stoke those embers. Throw some fodder on that bed of coals and get ready to see what will happen. Praise God the fire can never entirely go out, friend, because no one can snatch you from His strong and mighty hand (John 10:26–30). Be encouraged by that. If you have put your faith and trust in Christ alone for salvation, rest secure in that. The gift of eternal life extended to you through Christ was and is permanent. Remember, it is not based on your work but on His.

But the vibrancy of your faith? That's another topic. That's what we have been talking about in this book. If you find yourself in a salvation fire-funk, God wants you to escape it. He wants your salvation flame to be vibrant. He wants it hot and alive!

That's why I have challenged us in six areas. Again, this is *not* an exhaustive list. However, I have found that these are areas to assess, and when enacted, can get us out of spiritual dormancy. They will serve as a catalyst to a vibrant faith because I believe they are baseline activities and perspectives that move us to experience God. Yes, experience Him. And when you encounter Him, it forces reflection on who we are and who you are in Christ. Think of the six items we have discussed.

Rekindled Devotion—Bold Trust in God's Word
Note the experience:

Engaging God's Word is engaging God.

One of the most productive things we can do to revitalize our faith is to spend time with the Lord in His Word. We believe that "all Scripture is God-breathed" (2 Tim. 3:16 NIV). Remember walking through that? The words of the Bible are God's Words. He has spoken, and a way to jump-start our dead battery is simply to listen to what He has said. If you have not spent time with Him, allowing Him to transform your mind (Rom. 12:1–2), then the world speaks to your existence. Don't let the world teach you theology.

Rekindled Dependence—Total God-Reliance
Note the experience:

It's refrigerator trust. Submitting to Him reminds you of Who He is and, thus, who you are.

Living in total God-reliance keeps us in our place and reminds us that every day is a gift from God. We really can do nothing without Him. Our ability to breathe, work, create, and think is from Him. This experience keeps us in check. Call it what it is, friend. Sometimes, we think much more highly of ourselves than we should. A humble spirit of dependence also makes us give thanks for what He has done for us through Christ. He is God and you are not!

Rekindled Love—Authentic Compassion for Others
Note the experience:

Caring for others' well-being models His care for you.

Genuine concern for others models the life of Jesus. When we live in a spirit of compassion, many things occur. For starters, we are mimicking God Himself. Compassion is an attribute of God. God is "a compassionate and gracious God, slow to anger, abounding in love and faithfulness" (Ps. 86:15 NIV). Yet something happens when we display authentic compassion for others. It makes us grateful; it takes our eyes off ourselves, and allows us to see the world in need as God sees the world in need. When this occurs, sparks fly that will stir the coals of our hearts, igniting greater flames of faith.

Rekindled Holiness—Excellence in Character
Note the experience:

Giving Him your best expresses why you were created.

Character matters to God, and giving our best to Him is tied to knowing our purpose on the planet. God cares about the motives of our walk of faith—not just *what* we do. He cares about *how* we do it. Giving God our all to Him is an expression of acknowledging our purpose—being created in His image. God has given all image-bearers gifts. This general grace is extended to all humanity. But for those who recognize the Giver behind these gifts, that awareness becomes a source of purpose and power. Need to throw fuel on your fire? Strive to do everything with integrity of heart and skillfulness of hands (Ps. 78:72).

Rekindled Servanthood—Genuine Humility
Note the experience:

Servanthood mimics Jesus' life and avoids the pitfall of selfish ambition.

A life of servitude not only follows the life of Christ during His earthly ministry, but it models what He did by leaving heaven to become a man to die on the cross for our sins. Selfish ambition, present because of sin, focuses only on three people: me, myself, and I. However, as the apostle Paul states, "Don't look out only for your own interests, but take an interest in others, too" (Phil. 2:4). For in doing so, we adhere to the mandate of our Savior, to "love your neighbor as yourself" (Matt. 22:39). When we do this, our eyes are removed from self and motivated to love as God loves.

Rekindled Zeal—A Burden for the World
Note the experience:

Having a heart for the nations and all people aligns us with the heart of God.

God's heart for all people is clear. His love is not just for you and me. It's not just for our family, or our church, or those in our little group of friends. It's for all people. It's for broken people. It's people just like us. God's love is for the world. As John 3:16 states, "For this is how God loved the world: He gave his one and only Son, so that everyone who believes in him will not perish but have eternal life." Simply put, untold blessings are ours when we align to what matters most. God cares for people, not things.

As I have repeatedly stated, this is not an exhaustive list. Other items could be added, But I have found these to ignite a faith of fire. Yes, some of these are things "to do." However, they are not meant as a list of things to execute to see expected results. The human heart is at play here. Do things with the wrong motives, and nothing will change. Do them with a request to have a rekindled heart and I think God will shock you beyond your wildest dreams.

> *Now all glory to God, who is able, through his mighty power at work within us, to accomplish infinitely more than we might ask or think. Glory to him in the church and in Christ Jesus through all generations forever and ever! Amen.* (EPH. 3:20–21)

FINAL THOUGHTS TO WHOM IT APPLIES (YOU KNOW WHO YOU ARE)

Someone is likely reading this thinking, "I am too far into bad patterns to get my fire going again." Or, maybe you are thinking, "Yes, Mark, these things will help—but you don't know what I have done. You don't know the paths I have chosen or my decisions that have led to a smoldering, virtually nonexistent faith." Or someone may be thinking, "I have revitalized my faith on several occasions . . . and here I am again, seeing a minor trail of smoke where I should be seeing flames."

Good news: If any of those scenarios apply to you (or one of a thousand others that could be described), I have great news!

Jesus is in the restoration and reclamation business. It's His specialty.

A Session with Simon, a Lesson from the Lord

You are not the only one who has ever struggled with your faith. You are not the only one who thinks you have failed. Let's sit down and have a session with Simon Peter post-resurrection. To understand how Peter got schooled by Jesus after the cross, you need to remember who Peter was and what he said before the cross. Do you recall that three times he verbally denied even knowing Jesus?

Peter is a disciple with whom many of us can identify. We connect to his almost unbridled passion, a passion that is both admirable and troublesome. We first met Peter when Jesus called him into service. From what we know about Peter, he probably thought this invitation was something special for someone like himself who simply *was* special. That was Peter. He is described as bold and brave, always having the answer. On occasion, his faith shines. Remember the moment at Caesarea Philippi when Jesus asked the disciples, "Who do people say that the Son of Man is?" (Matt. 16:13). All the disciples chimed in on that one. It's easy to relay the scuttlebutt of the community. However, when Jesus zeroed in on those right there in eye contact, the anxiety level in the circle went up. Jesus said, "But who do *you* say I am?" (v. 15; emphasis added). I can't prove it to you, but I am guessing all the disciples started staring at doodle bugs on the ground and suddenly had to retie their sandals. After some time, Peter broke the silence. His words were divinely brilliant. He said, "You are the Messiah, the Son of the living God" (Matt. 16:16).

Peter received a gold star for that reply, which, as Jesus said, was revealed by God the Father. Peter's beautiful confession is the rock on which the church is built—for all who believe and confess that Jesus is God's promised Messiah, the very Son of the living God. Good job, Peter. What a stalwart moment of faith!

Keep reading. In the following passage of Scripture, Jesus predicts His death, and Peter, in essence, said, "No sir, Jesus. That ain't gonna happen on my watch." Then Jesus said to Peter, "Get away from me, Satan. You are a dangerous trap to me. You are seeing things merely from a human point of view, not from God's" (Matt.16:23) Ouch. That one had to sting Peter a bit. He went from being an "A" pupil to being called the devil. Well, that's Peter! That's why he is called ol' open mouth, insert foot, Pete. And if we're honest, most of us can relate to him. In Peter, we see ourselves.

Peter had another brash moment that would come back to bite him. In John 13, on the night of Jesus' betrayal, our Lord met with his disciples and told them of the cross to come and that He would soon be leaving and returning to the Father. In response to Jesus saying, "You can't go with me now" (v. 36), Peter blurted out, "But why can't I come now, Lord?…I'm ready to die for you" (v. 37). To that, Jesus answered, "Die for me? I tell you the truth, Peter—before the rooster crows tomorrow morning, you will deny three times that you even know me" (v. 38).

I'm not going to recount the details of that story for you—but that is precisely what happened. In John 18:15–27, Peter, huddling around a charcoal fire, denied Jesus not once, but three times. Peter denied he even knew Jesus, lying and betraying the Lord just as Judas had done. Judas betrayed him for money; Peter betrayed Him out of fear. Either way, Peter's faith was crushed and dimmed. Dimmed, but not destroyed. Our Lord, post-resurrection, was about to do what only He can do. Remember? Jesus is in the restoration and reclamation business.

Fast-forward to the biblical story. Jesus went to the cross, conquered death, and exited the grave. In a resurrected state, Jesus appeared to the women at the tomb, to Peter, Cleopas and another disciple on their way to Emmaus, the ten disciples (minus Thomas), and again to all eleven. It's there that our momentous story continues. Jesus appeared next to seven disciples by the Sea of Galilee. This time, He doesn't just appear to them, He chose to have an extended time of restoration and reclamation with his friend Peter, the man who had denied Him *three* times.

In John 21, we find several disciples (Peter, Thomas, Nathanael, James, John, and "two others") fishing, but the episode seems to be focused on Peter. Not only was he mentioned first in the list of names, but Peter had also returned to his previous occupation. "I'm going fishing," Peter says (v. 3). As the account records, they did that. They fished, but they didn't catch anything.

Early in the morning—their expedition changed. In this post-resurrection account, Jesus shows up and instructs them to "Throw out your net on the right-hand side of the boat, and you'll get some!" (v. 6). The disciples had been in this situation before (Luke 5:5–11), but they obeyed the risen Savior and had a record catch—153 fish, to be exact.

When Peter understood that the one giving the instructions was Jesus, he jumped into the water and scampered ashore to see him, leaving the record catch in the hands of his compadres. He found Jesus preparing breakfast by cooking over a charcoal fire; a fire reminiscent of the one earlier where he stood warming himself with Roman guards as he *denied* knowing Jesus.

While the text does not say so, this charcoal fire must have triggered regrets in Peter's mind. He had failed. His faith had dwindled. The vibrant fire that he had expressed on other occasions was now dormant. By all practical assessment, while Peter was thankful for the Lord's resurrection, his faith remained passive, so much so that he had returned to his old livelihood of fishing.

Once you've met Jesus, you are never normal. He is focused on calling you to something higher—even after you have betrayed Him.

After the boat landed with the fish, Jesus instructed the others to bring more fish for the fire. As Jesus fed them breakfast, they ate, perhaps in stunned silence. The text reminds the reader, "None of the disciples dared to ask him, 'Who are you?' They knew it was the Lord" (John 21:12).

When the meal was over, Jesus spoke to Peter. But it is not just casual conversation. He addresses *the* issue, the proverbial elephant in the room. My friend Chuck Swindoll says, "As if to take Peter back to the beginning, before he was "the Rock," Jesus looked across the charcoal fire and addressed the dejected disciple. . . . The time had come for Jesus to address Peter's deepest wound."[1]

Moments with the Lord are always tender, and Peter's breakfast encounter was no different. In three questions over a charcoal fire, Jesus asks Peter if he loves Him. Did you hear it? Jesus asks Peter three times if he loved Him, to which Peter said, "Yes!" Jesus asks him over a charcoal fire. Jesus reenacts Peter's denials to restore him. Don't miss it. As Edwin Blum says, "Three times Peter said he did not even know the Lord (18:17, 25, 27); now three times he said he loved the Lord (21:15-17). No matter how great a person is, he may fall. But God's grace and forgiveness will restore the repentant."[2]

He will restore your dormant fire of faith if you let Him. Your story may not be a denial. It may not be a failure. It may simply be carelessness or negligence. Whatever your story, He longs to restore and reclaim your walk of faith. So let Jesus do His thing. He will do it. And when He does, and when you let Him . . .

Watch out for the roar of the flame.

ACKNOWLEDGMENTS

No book is written in isolation. The hands of many touch such a work and form it into its final product—always making it better—and I am grateful for all the hands that went into this one, to be sure. And don't forget: All writers steal from other thieves! Voices of the past spill forward through expressions, illustrations, and stories.

I would be remiss without giving thanks to many. Out of the shoot, I desire to applaud the collaborative and editing efforts of Mark Tobey, a gifted writer, thinker, and communicator. Thank you for pouring into this project with a winsome and contagious spirit. As you have experienced many challenges along this publishing journey, I have observed a deep faith that matches them. You encourage me, friend.

Appreciation is extended for the editing eye of my precious wife, Jennifer. Your thoughts are always spot-on. Thanks for helping me see that others don't always understand what I think I am saying! I am also grateful for the insights of my parents, Bob and Janet Yarbrough. Every book I have ever written has their indelible influence.

Let me also give a big, giant thank-you to our friends at Moody Publishers. It has been a pleasure working with you on this project. Specifically, I would like to thank Drew Dyck and Pam Pugh. Your efforts have led the charge. Keep at it, friends.

Finally, I would like to thank the entire team at Dallas Theological Seminary. Specifically, thank you to my Executive Team for the discussion on core values. This book adapts many dialogues on that topic and frames our values in a larger context for all believers. In that regard, I would also like to thank Jalen Lee, who provided creativity in chapel messages on this topic.

Last, I would like to cheer on those who need a rekindled heart. Don't quit, friends. Let our Great God stoke your fire of faith. He will bring the heat if you let Him! To God be the glory.

NOTES

Chapter 1: Rekindled Devotion: Bold Trust in God's Word

1. Elvina M. Hall, "Jesus Paid It All," 1865, https://hymnary.org/text/i_hear_the_savior_say_thy_strength_indee.
2. Warren Wiersbe, *The Bible Exposition Commentary, Vol. 2* (Victor Books, 1996), 253.

Chapter 2: Rekindled Dependence: Total God-Reliance

1. *Merriam-Webster,* s.v. "everything (*n3;*)," https://www.merriam-webster.com/dictionary/everything.
2. Charles Dickens, *A Christmas Carol* (Chapman & Hall, 1843), 1.
3. Robert Robinson, "Come, Thou Fount, of Every Blessing," 1758, https://hymnary.org/text/come_thou_fount_of_every_blessing.

Chapter 3: Rekindled Love: Authentic Compassion for Others

1. *Guinness World Records 2023* (Guinness World Record Limited, The Jim Pattison Group, 2022).
2. C. S. Lewis, "Weight of Glory," sermon, University Church of St. Mary the Virgin, Oxford, June 8, 1941.

Chapter 4: Rekindled Holiness: Excellence in Character

1. Popularly adapted from Robert Burns (1759–1796), "To a Mouse," 1785. Burns's actual line in this poem reads: "The best-laid schemes o' mice an' men gang aft agley."

Chapter 5: Rekindled Servanthood: Genuine Humility

1. Scholars debate the authorship of Hebrews. If Paul is the writer of this epistle, he would have written fourteen books of the New Testament.

2. Craig Brian Larson, *750 Engaging Illustrations for Preachers, Teachers, and Writers* (Baker Publishing Group, 2007), 309.

Chapter 6: Rekindled Zeal: A Burden for the World

1. James D. G. Dunn, *The Epistles to the Colossians and to Philemon: A Commentary on the Greek Text,* New International Greek Testament Commentary (William B. Eerdmans Publishing; Paternoster Press, 1996), 205.
2. William Barclay, *The Letters to the Philippians, Colossians and Thessalonians,* The Daily Study Bible Series, 2nd ed. (Saint Andrew Press, 1963), 177.

The End . . . But Only the Beginning

1. Charles R. Swindoll, *Swindoll's New Testament Insight: Insights on John* (Zondervan: 2014), 354.
2. Edwin A. Blum, "John," in *The Bible Knowledge Commentary: An Exposition of the Scriptures,* ed. J. F. Walvoord and R. B. Zuck, vol. 2 (Victor Books, 1985), 345.

Joy—our lifeline and strength through life's suffering.

From the Word to Life

Chip Ingram takes us to God's Word, helping us shift away from self-centric happiness and toward lasting joy found in God's goodness. You cannot choose life's circumstances, but you can choose how to respond. Join esteemed teacher Chip Ingram on this journey to restore the essential Christian virtue of JOY!

Also available as an eBook

Tozer's bestseller, this book has been called "one of the all-time most inspirational books" by a panel of Christian magazine writers.

From the Word to Life

The Pursuit of God is a Christian classic about reclaiming God's presence in a clamoring world. Bringing the mystics to bear on modern spirituality, A.W. Tozer raises high our thoughts of God, makes low our love for the world, and draws our gaze to the heights of heaven.

Also available as an eBook and an audiobook